UNIVERSITY MONOGRAPH SERIES

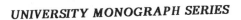

THROWING THE STICKS

Occult Self-Therapy

THE ARTS OF SELF-TRANSCENDENCE

IN POST-FREUDIAN MODES OF THOUGHT

John Charles Cooper, Ph.D.

Professor of Religion

Susquehanna University

WYNDHAM HALL PRESS

# THROWING THE STICKS

Occult Self-Therapy

## THE ARTS OF SELF-TRANSCENDENCE

## IN POST-FREUDIAN MODES OF THOUGHT

by

John Charles Cooper, Ph.D.
Professor of Religion
Susquehanna University

Library of Congress
Catalog Card Number:

85-051340

ISBN    0-932269-49-4

# DEDICATION

For Katie and Nathan Bender who helped

and for all those who shared.

Blessed Be.

# TABLE OF CONTENTS

# PREFACE

Some years ago there was a popular song whose refrain ran, "Is that all there is?" The lyrics asked more than the usual quest for romance over sensuality or for responsibility over romance alone. It asked if eating and sleeping, loving and working were all there were to life. The song, consciously or unconsciously, pointed to the roots of the religious consciousness; to humankind's longing for transcendence, for a state of consciousness that lies above and beyond the world. Even in the reactionary eighties that longing for transcendence is still strong. While many people have attempted to quench their thirst for the "more" in the midst of the world in literalist religiousity; many others have been turned off and left unsatisfied by demands to acquiese to the religious claims of others. To be born again, to become a twice born person, is the road to self-transcendence, but it can not be a second hand experience undergone in the same way as others. To experience a new life, genuinely, is a unique experience. The search for self-transcendence, then, is part of the search for, and the discovery of, the self. As always, the mantic, occult, hidden arts and interests flourish in the eighties, since the primacy of the self and its desires is key to occultism. We may think it strange that people who use electricity and are familiar with nuclear power still believe in the stars, but it is precisely people who have plumbed the depths of the material world and still feel a spiritual lack who are most apt to search for "something more" in the dark side of the human tradition; in the hidden world of the occult.

This monograph is a report on the occult elements in America's popular religious culture, forming a continuation to my RELIGION IN THE AGE OF AQUARIUS (Westminster Press, 1971).

I wish to express my appreciation to the Popular Culture Association, Indianapolis, Indiana, on April 13-15, 1973. A portion of Chapter I was read in the section "Social Dimensions of the Occult", chaired by Robert Galbreath, of the Center for Twentieth Century Studies at the University of Wisconsin, Milwaukee. Some of the material also was given as lectures to seminars in the Department of Psychiatry,

1

The Medical College of Louisiana, in 1975. Thanks are due, too, to the Seminar on Occult Studies of The American Academy of Religion, which I served as Chairman, 1975-76.

This book is designed as an aid to clergymen, teachers, church school teachers, humanistic psychologists, Jungians, parents and others who find themselves with persons attracted to the occult among whom self-therapy has come to a high state of development in our time.

# INTRODUCTION

## THE SEARCH FOR SELF-KNOWLEDGE

From the beginnings of time men have sought counsel and guidance for themselves. Faced with the manifold problems of life, with illness, harsh weather, food shortages, wild animals, war and the inevitability of death, people of every age have sought to marshall all the inward strengths they have and to overcome their inner weaknesses. Men and women sensed that they must get themselves "together" in order to enhance their chances of survival in the face of a difficult natural environment and an often pitiless social situation. Many scholars have stressed the emergence of astrology, the primal mythological archetypes and eventually religion and philosophy from man's attempts to understand and control their natural environment. Faced with the immensity of the universe, men sought for signs that would guide their present and future actions. Undoubtedly this facing of the exteior dimension of reality is part of the development of man's occultic, later religious and much later philosophical methods and systems. Aristotle remarks upon this exterior, cosmological interest in the development of philosophy in the METAPHYSICS. Yet Aristotle also rehearses the history of philosophy up to his time, stressing the wise men, including Socrates, who sought first to know themselves. I want to develop here the interior dimension of the religious-philosophical quest, which is as basic to humanistic psychology and to religious practices today as they have been from the foundations of civilization.

People today look at the rods cast to create the hexagrams of the **I-Ching,** at the patterns formed by **The Tarot** and even regular playing cards, at their palms, the numerical equivalent of their names, at the pattern of the heavens at the moments of their births -- all taken as clues to their characters and solutions to felt problems. This is a form of psychotherapy that I call post-Freudian self-therapy. For those who use the Bible, the Prayer Book or the rosary in their self-searching, I use the term religious self-therapy. Since we would

3

consider it normal, in such a Judeo-Christian influenced society, for persons to turn to religious sources for personal help, I will not pursue an analysis of this practice here. I will rather turn to the more unusual, but growing, practices of self-therapy based on non-Biblical material and attempt to assess the significance of this phenomenon for organized religion and for our common society.

Psychotherapy, we are just beginning to realize, only does in a formal way the healing activity that many traditional institutions, roles and activities do for people in a society that is spiritually alive.

People have always recognized the truth of this with regard to many of the functions of the traditional church. Confession, contrition and absolution; public worship, fellowship, and private counseling, all these activities of institutional religion, have psychotherapeutic effects. The expression of one's feelings of guilt and shortcomings and the acceptance of the person despite their past and present negative aspects is healing and mental health enhancing. A little reflection convinces us of the overlapping of religious beliefs and activities and the field of psychology.

But we do not, as often, recognize the psychotherapeutic aspects of other social activities. Today the therapeutic role of poetry, both its writing and its study, is being recognized. The therapeutic effects of sports activities were much overvalued for generations, on the other hand. Today, we are recognizing that sports don't necessarily contribute to sound minds in sound bodies, while poetry, literature, drama and music may actually contribute to one's mental health. Of course, Aristotle recognized the cathartic, emotionally cleansing function of drama 2400 years ago.

The various practices we usually call the occult, however, have generally not been identified with a psychotherapeutic function, except by those in occult circles, and then not in psychological terms. It is a fact, nevertheless, that occult practices do often function as both psychoanalytic and psychoterapeutic tools. Men and women use the paraphenalia and the practices of the occult to plumb the depths of their minds, evaluate their past experiences and purge the guilts and fears that plague their minds. Even those familiar (in a sociological or literary sense) with the practice of magic forget that not only do witches cast spells to harm, but also spells to heal. People read their horoscopes, and pay well to have them cast, precisely to gain insight into themselves and to guide their future behavior. I don't think the therapeutic usage of occult practices can be denied.

4

This is a book about the psychoanalytic and psychotherapeutic use of occultic techniques as self-therapy. It is not about strange people from far away but about housewives, professors, students, sales clerks, physicians and servicemen in the United States here and now. Welcome to that unexpected adjunct to the community mental health program, the self-therapy underground.

Susquehanna University

Selinsgrove, Pennsylvania

John C. Cooper

1985

# CHAPTER I

## THE POST FREUDIAN SITUATION

### The Occult is Part of Our Life

Not long ago I was lecturing on my book, RELIGION IN THE AGE OF AQUARIUS,[1] at a small college. We had gathered to talk and drink coffee. The college host turned to me and said, "There's a young lady sitting there in a modified lotus position who has something she might want to tell us." I turned and looked at a dark, quite small young lady who had been sitting quietly in a loose, yoga-like pose all during the previous conversations. She began to talk, speaking softly. "I've been on the Tibetan death trip, you know, through all the Buddhist Bardos?" I answered, "Yes, you mean the descent through the hells?" "Yes," she responded, "all the way to where I was ripped apart."

"How Long ago was this?"

"Eight months ago."

"Were you alone?"

"No, I was with my friend, J. M., who was interested in getting his head straight, since he had been up on drugs for some time."

"Have you been up on drugs?"

"No. Never."

"How long had you meditated and followed Buddhist studies?"

"I began, with J. M., at 6:00 p.m. I don't know when I slipped into the visions, but they were over by 4:00 a.m."

"What did you see?"

"My own death. I saw myself ripped apart, dead. Then I passed from one vision of a Bardo (hell) to another. Some were awful, gross. Some were not so bad and gave me relief. When I came out of it, I was at peace and knew I had to decide whether to drop the whole thing or to enter a (Buddhist) monastery. I fell into a fever trying to come to a decision. Eventually, I fell asleep and when I awoke, J. M. was gone. He had left a note saying he wouldn't wait and had gone to Detroit to enter the Buddhist monastery there."

"What did you do?"

"I decided I had got all I needed out of 'meditation' and abandoned it."

This young lady went on to say that she had recently returned to a form of "scientific meditation" and was continuing in it.

## Occultic Science

The occult has been considered "unscientific" only since the nineteenth century. In the days of the French Revolution, and after, what would pass today as occultism or medical "quackery" was the rage in France. Only with the building up of data and method and prestige in the several branches of physical and social studies in the nineteenth century did the various areas of occultism come to be read out of "science." We are generally not told of the supremely religious ends that the great Newton wished his physical theories to accomplish. We are not told that Galileo and other great astronomers cast horoscopes on the side to make their living.

Yet in the Renaissance era, there were five, not one, occult sciences. the systems included astrology, white magic, witchcraft, alchemy and the mystical philosophy of Hermes Trismegistus.[2] Perhaps the sign of the Renaissance likeness of our present age is the acceptance of the claim of the occult to be a science by millions of people.

It undoubtedly seems strange to many people to speak of the occult and psychotherapy or psychoanalysis in the same statement. One is accustomed to thinking of psychoanalysis as a branch of medicine, of science. One is also accustomed to thinking of occultism as referring to a nonscientific, perhaps even a pathological phenomena, among a small number of people. However, we are living in a strange period

8

of time, a period when people are lost, not just in the sense of confusion, but in some spiritual sense of lostness, in which they have lost all contact with the traditional reference points and standards for their lives. Therefore, they find themselves caught up in the dizziness that the Existentialist philosopher, Jean Paul Sartre, has termed nausea. This dizziness reflects itself in the 1980's in an ever increasingly dynamic search for any guide to conduct, for any standard by which to measure our behavior, for any means with which to reach wholeness and happiness in life.

This period has seen the widespread dissemination of popular knowledge about psychology and peculiarly of psychoanalysis. The rather old-fashioned terminology of Freud is used throughout our culture. Moreover, the parallel terminology of Reich, of Adler, and of other psychologists and psychiatrists, is also well known. The psychology-system of the psychiatrist, Carl Jung, of Switzerland, which has some grounding in occultic topics, such as astrology and mysticism, is widespread, and is rather pervasive in the literature and creative fields of our day. Anyone familiar with the writings of Carl Gustav Jung would not find the bringing together of the terms "occult" and "psychotherapy" unusual.

Millions of the Americans who are interested in astrology, spiritualism and the occult in general are not aware of the interest in occult matters which filled the life of Jung. Jung's belief in the reality of occult phenomena caused him to break off his close association with the founder of modern psychiatry, Sigmund Freud.

Jung, in his autobiography, recounts an incident of the reality of the occult in his life which disturbed and irritated Freud. It appars that Freud wished men to make an unquestioned dogma out of his theory of the sexual basis of mental disturbances. Jung resisted this dogmatism, and was told by Freud that the sexual theory was a wall to keep out the black tide of occultism. While Jung and Freud were arguing, there was a sudden, sharp noise in the bookcase next to them. Jung recognized it as the sign of a poltergeist or spirit. When he told Freud this, Freud laughed and called such an explanation rubbish. Jung replied that his explanation was not rubbish and predicted that the uncanny noise would happen again. The noise immediately rang out like a cannon shot. Freud looked frightened and amazed and remained silent.[3]

Nevertheless, we generally do not think of occultism, meaning here the casting of horoscopes, of astrology, palmistry, the casting of fortunes by means of Tarot cards, and other similar mystical practices, as being psychoanalytic and therapeutic in any direct sense. but it is the case that the increasing popularity of these activities is due not just to their esoteric attraction, but because more and more people are finding in them ways in which they believe they have truthful analyses of their characters and helpful guides by which to pattern their future conduct. Any art by which a person determines their characteristics, fastens upon some idea of their character, and guides their future conduct and behavior, must be considered psychoanalytic, and indeed often psychotherapeutic, in the sense of the dissolution of mental and emotional problems.

The last two decades have seen the growth of the community mental health center. It has also seen a very widespread growth of private psychologists and counseling situations; it has witnessed the rise of more accomplished training in psychological counseling by the clergy, and the spread throughout the public school system of school psychologists and counselors. More and more, at every level, certainly not ignoring industry and business, psychology has become a tool of management, of education, of the armed forces and of the government at all levels. But despite this fact most people with problems of an emotional or psychiatric nature, do not get psychological treatment or help. We are still faced with the fact that community health centers and family counseling services generally find that people who are ultimately referred to them go to clergymen first, if they are lucky enough to seek out any kind of responsible help at all. We would be surprised and shocked to learn that millions of people had not been treated for the disease of smallpox, but we are not surprised to know that there are walking wounded, psychiatrically speaking, on every street. Despite the growing availability of psychological counseling services, many people are not being reached.

In this very same period of time, over the last quarter century, we have also seen the growth of many esoteric religious traditions in America. These new religious cults and new approaches to religion very often show all the earmarks of movements designed to meet the psychological needs of people who have lost their bearings, lost their social roots, and lost their ability to respond positively to traditional forms of religion. We should not be surprised to learn that many of these new religious ideas and movements have at least one of their feet in traditional esoteric ideas that have been rightly or wrongly called occultic. Spirits, demons, spiritualism, faith healing, exorcisms, visions, auditions and revelations make up the warp and woof of many of the new religions, often called cults, in North America.

10

## Anti-intellectualism in the Age of Aquarius

For a long time the so-called hard sciences of physics and chemistry and their related fields developed at an amazing pace. In something like the last 35 years, the "soft-sciences" of sociology and psychology have experienced the same explosive growth that characterized physics in the earlier part of the century. We know there has been a kind of internal revulsion in many minds against the "hard sciences" in our time. In a time when we are increasingly aware of the ability of the hard sciences to provide the technologists with data that makes all kinds of improvements and possibilities available to the general public through the mass productive process, there has been a turning away from and lack of respect for the hard sciences themselves. The fact that science has been able to produce more and better weapons of death, has been able to pollute the surface of the earth and the very atmosphere itself at a fantastic rate, as well as providing us with computers and jet planes, may have something to do with this. I feel that one of the things that we are experiencing now and will continue to experience at a greater rate in the near future is a parallel revulsion against the soft sciences (social sciences) on the part of the public as well. It could be argued that while we are experiencing a tremendous popularity of psychology, there has been a parallel revulsion against the notion of psychology, that is the study of the mind or soul, as a science. The movement that has established humanistic psychology as the thirty-second definable branch of psychology recognized by the American Psychological Association, tends to concretize within the field of psychology itself a turning away from the experimentalism and the models of the machine and of the efficient organism that characterized modern psychology up until the present time. I dare say that the turning to occult practices, with their heavy overtones of superstition, their anti-rationalism and their appeal to ceremony and ritual, may represent an even more severe turning away from psychology, which perhaps too carefully and too insistently sought to establish itself as a "science."

If it sounds strange to speak of a revolt against psychology as a science, it will not sound as strange because it has so often been declared, to speak of revolt against religion as an established modality in our society. We are aware, both on the popular as well as on the social level, of the real revolt against traditional organized religion. The Bureau of the Census figures since approximately 1961 have shown a steadily declining rate of attendance at services and of memberships in church bodies. These are absolute rather than relative figures, i.e., they are not relative to the population's growth. At the same time we have witnessed the growth of some unusual forms of theology, which often have been actually ill-disguised criticisms of the church and of the church's theological position, from within the churches' own ranks.

We must note in connection with this consideration, that the clergy over the past quarter century has become, on the whole, more and more adept at personal counseling. There has been a steady moving away from the older tradition of moralism and of moral homilies on the part of clergymen in their relating to parishioners, and also away from a simple confession-absolution relationship on the part of priests and parishioners, towards a more flexible and more open form of encounter with real possibilities for human growth and development. Great credit should be given to the seminaries and universities and outstanding pastor-professors there who have introduced many scientific and medical forms of personal counseling and analysis to the theologians. However, we may now be finding a revolt against this. The church has not historically been a leader of thought in the West since the Renaissance. Now we can see that the revolution in the field of psychology had been started long before it became a popular topic for clergymen to discuss. It may be that the church will continue to be offering kinds of counseling and other psychological services that will have to be abandoned by the professional psychiatric and psychological fields, simply because of this cultural lag on the part of the ecclesiastical institution.

In any event, we may see the rise of do-it-yourself, self-therapy as a mute reaction to and rejection of both the counseling services of the church on the one hand, and the scientific behaviorism of B. F. Skinner and the experimental psychologists on the other.

I am concerned here with offering some descriptions of various self-therapy techniques that are presently being practiced in America. I am not concerned with giving a history of occultism, and its practices, nor will I talk about occultic techniques that may have been prominent in past eras. I am interested in those techniques that are discernable among the population in the United States and Canada at the present time. I will then attempt to assess these occultic techniques for any possible usefulness they might have in a psychotherapeutic relationship. I have it on the authority of a large number of people that are involved in occultic practices, that they do, indeed, seek to help people understand their characters, and seek to dissolve or to solve the kind of mental or emotional problems that these

12

people show to them when they come to them for their ministrations. I will be illustrating each of the techniques with examples drawn from life, showing how people with problems come to occultic leaders and how these occultic leaders attempt to help them in their distress. I will speak honestly of the cases in which the distresses were not alleviated, and will speak also with complete honesty, insofar as I am able to ascertain the truth, about cases of distress that were helped by these strange, unscientific practices.

I am concerned with psychotherapeutics, that is, the healing of mind and spirit, in the widest possible sense of that word. I will pay attention to the attempts of human beings to use occultic practices to help them to deal more fruitfully and humanely with their environment. I will deal with occult practices as they are used to help people to deal more sanely with the often confused and callous political situation in the United States. I will show the attempts to use occultic practices by large numbers of people as a way of exorcising the bad influences they feel impinging upon their lives. I shall definitely mention the exorcism of the Pentagon in 1967; the situation recorded so graphically by Norman Mailer in THE ARMIES OF THE NIGHT.[4] I shall call upon people for eyewitness information about this practice. I will show a possible overlapping of the mysticism that underlies occultism and the kind of pantheistic mysticism that underlies the deep concern for the environment in our day. I think of Earth Day and the celebration of the goodness of the earth that man has so viciously raped and destroyed as akin to the mysticism which underlies occultism. In short, I will atempt to take a look at this all pervasive movement of mystic religiosity in our day, as it is related to, and as it is sociologically caused by, the many profound dilemmas we have gotten ourselves into, politically, socially, religiously, emotionally and most of all, intellectually.

**The Search for the Self**

A physician-friend of mine who has practiced psychiatry for many years reported to me that he has encountered patients in whom the interest in occultism has proved a means of finding better mental health. A letter from him says,

". . . I have found in several patients that their study of astrology has helped them begin to overcome their egocentricity and self-sufficiency in that they have learned to accept the idea that there are or may be forces from without that influence their lives and that this force is beyond their control. This is the road that at least two patients have traveled in coming back to their acceptance of a Supreme Being."[5]

This physician's remarks are underscored by Dr. E. Mansell Pattison, Assistant Professor of Psychiatry and Coordinator for Social and Community Psychiatry at the University of Washington School of Medicine, Seattle. Dr. Pattison presented a paper entitled "Witchcraft and Psychiatry Working Side by Side" at the 125th Convention of the American Psychiatric Association in 1972.

Dr. Pattison observed that cultures in transition, such as the developing nations, exhibit a parallelism of faith healers and ordinary medical work side and side. He declares that people go to one or the other of these types of healers on the basis of their assessment of the cause of their discomfort. Pattison says that if the person feels that his illness, for example, the common cold, is caused by his having been sinful, he will seek out a faith healer, but if he feels the colds is a result of having been out in the rain, he will go to a regular medical doctor.

Pattison gives as an example a case of a young girl in an American Indian tribe who fell ill with a mysterious hysteria although she was a twentieth-century youngster, doing well in high school. He was called in on the case and asked the girl's mother what would have been done for the girl in the old days. The mother replied that they would have let the girl wander in the wilderness to wrestle with the demons. Pattison observes that this was similar to the story recorded in the Old Testament where Jacob wrestled with the angel and obtains a blessing, although he is injured by the encounter. (Genesis 32: 22-32) Pattison suggested that it would be better to attempt to exorcise the girl by the old rituals. They found that the girl's grandmother knew this procedure. She performed the ceremony and the girl was healed.[6]

One might ask what relevance this occurrence in an American Indian family has to do with the rest of us? I would answer, much, because we live in a transitional culture today that is already showing the stresses and strains of a dying older culture and a new culture coming to life. In our present situation we are not greatly different from the situation of an American Indian family making the transition from older tribal ways to a new world view or of a developing African nation where one culture is breaking down under the influence of another. Such cultural shock may very well explain the development of witchcraft and faith healing to high levels in our day.

Dr. Samuel Laeuchli of Temple University has observed that "If religion disappears in the modern world, man will look to magic for his hopes and aspirations." Speaking before the Temple University student body on June 17, 1970, Laeuchli declared: "Our society incresingly demonstrates that it seeks magic as a fulfillment of life -- astrology and voodoo being examples of the trend."[7]

Laeuchli feels that the organized churches are in a state of terrible conflict between those who wish to hold on to the conservative security they have in the old time religion and those who feel that religion simply must change to take account of the new situation of the world. He seems to feel that if the churches do not change the majority of people will simply forego classical religion. His estimate of what would happen then is: "When you take away this classical religion from man, he will turn either to astrology and magic for the fulfillment of his dreams, or seek a greater consciousness of the religious past in the poetic and historical perspectives."[8]

## The Search for Self-Healing

Sitting in one's home or office in the 1980's listening to the radio, looking at the television, reading the newspapers and news magazines, while studying the practices and beliefs of the occult, one falls in to a wild, schizophrenic state of mind. Truthfully, the wider social scene in North America seems as strange and illogical to an objective observer as does the smaller scene of occultism. It is not strange to me that occultism flourishes in times like these. Uncertainty, anxiety, rootlessness, restlessness are the social atmosphere we inhabit. People cannot abide this unremitting anxiety, they cannot be philosophical and see that everything changes but change itself. Men turn to the meaning and guidance promised in occultic practice precisely for relief from this intolerable state of psychic strain.

How is it possible that men and women find counsel about their innermost selves through the use of I-Ching, coins and sticks, Tarot cards, astrology charts and the lines in their hands? That people do receive self insight and even experience a healing of emotional disturbances is a fact, as our illustrations drawn from the actual case histories of a psychiatrist demonstrate. Actually, there are several explanations possible, some of them of a religious, others of a psychological nature.

Self-therapy is not only a search for self, and for the healing of self, but like religion, with which it must be compared, it is also a search for self-transcendence. The occult always has self-improvement, a moral or gain in mind as it undertakes its study and practices. Occultic belief arises when men begin to feel that there is something wrong with them as they naturally stand and that they need to be changed. In the past occultism was associated with science as well as religion. Today, it seems to be associated with another strong interest of the counter culture, science fiction. Ray Bradbury, a noted science fiction writer, has declared that science fiction is the only place philosophy can be done in our day. The famous founder of science fiction writing, Jules Verne, was quite interested in the occult as far back as the nineteenth century.

From another side, humanistic psychology is very interested in the occult in our day. it is difficult to separate some of the sensitivity groups and occultic groups from each other. G. I. Gurdjieff, speaking of the need to awaken to what we really are and what the present situation in the world really is, has said:

"In order for the spirit to awaken, a combination of efforts is needed. It is necessary that somebody should look after the man who wakes him; it is necessary to have alarm clocks and it is also necessary continually to invent new alarm clocks. But in order to achieve all this and to obtain results, a certain number of people must work together. One man can do nothing."[9]

In assessing the possible working of occultism in the process of finding and healing the self, we must note that, first, occult therapy rests at least on the same basis as faith healing as practiced in the organized churches. Quite a few respected leaders preach: "All things are possible if you only believe." Perhaps not all things, but a great many things are. Occult self-therapy also rests on the same foundations as pastoral counseling, teacher advice, mutual reinforcement of one another by friends and all the other thousands of healing acts that take place everyday. Occult psychotherapy undoubtedly rests on faith -- and faith has pragmatic "cash value" (in William James' terms) in the solutions of the problems of life.

I recognize that in the counseling and healing process a number of things are going on, including a process of clarification by means of whatever method is invoked; a form of auto-suggestion may be instituted and a gestalt may be set up into which one is enabled to project the deepest feelings of the subconscious about his problem,

16

and translate them into the activities of the group. The other group members and the cards, charts, etc. may simply serve as reinforcers of this method of self-analysis or as aids to concentration. I will not say that this is all that is involved in faith healing, whether under traditional religious or occultic conditions, but regardless of what else may be involved, at least this much of the psychodynamic process is included. If the person has faith in the tenets of the group, again either religious or occultic, the possibility is greatly increased that he or she will accept the insights so gained and incorporate them in his/her life.

It is generally accepted that human beings search for transcendence. Men and women feel their limitations and long to overcome them. Such a feeling of dissatisfaction with self is not a mark of mental disturbance but of a realistic recognition of the shortcomings and failures we all are heir to in life. However, Jean Paul Sartre has given us an interesting counter view of transcendence. Sartre suggests that human beings seek transcendence because of their bad faith. Bad faith for Sartre, means the capacity men have to deceive themselves, their desire to escape from themselves and from the factual state of their being-in-the-world.[10]

Sartre has also attacked Sigmund Freud and Freud's concept of the unconscious which is supposed to provide an explanation of our motivations and desires. Sartre goes so far as to say the Freud is engaging in sympathetic magic when he postulates the existence of the unconscious.[11]

Sartre may well be right about Freud's use of occultic material rebaptized with psychological names. He may even be right about certain human predispositions to seek transcendence. After all, the book of Genesis ascribes the fall of mankind into sin to Eve's, and then Adam's, desire to transcend themselves by becoming wise, knowing good from evil (Genesis 3: 1-24).

Sartre's question as to whether the search for transcendence is an example of bad faith or not is one to which we must pay heed. Mythology and fairy tales, which represent the deposit of traditional wisdom, give us many examples of persons who over-reach themselves and destroy themselves because of their ruthless drive for transcendence. The story of Icarus, who flew too close to the sun, is a prime example. The Christian tradition has always held that man's basic sin is the desire to be like God and expresses itself in rebellion against God.

17

It may be that we have to learn to distinguish between various kinds of transcendence. A transcendence that is basically a selfish search and a transcendence that comes through a willing submission to God, must be distinguished from each other.

The question might be put in another way. Does man suffer because he aspires, or does he aspire because he suffers? This book rests on the thesis that the second half of this question is true. Because of the sufferings we experience in our disjointed world and the abdication of the element of mystery in modern religion, men seek their aspirations more and more in the occult. Even a Catholic priest, Richard Woods, O.P., has recognized the occult as the counter cultural religion. He sees positive elements in this occultism as well as dangerous ones. He says:

"Religious interest in modern occultism can warrant theological investigation, replete with sociological insights and psychological theories. It may also take the form of pastoral concern. While distinct, the pastoral dimension should in this case (as in all others, I hasten to add) be rooted in a theological and socio-scientific appraisal of the situation, lest more harm than good result from well-meant but futile accusations, harangues and rescue missions. There is doubtless an element of moral and even phsycial danger in occultism, but it is worse than useless to assault the matter frontally, for what harm there is operates behind a phalanx of socio-psychological fringe benefits that are of tangible worth to those involved."[12]

There are dangers involved in occultism, some of which I pointed out in my book, RELIGION IN THE AGE OF AQUARIUS.[13] We will discuss further the dangers as we analyze the occultic practices that are used for self-analysis. But nevertheless, call it what we will; sympathetic magic, unconscious forces, repressions, resistances, vibrations, human attractions, sex appeal, charisma, presences, impressiveness, fascination, repulsion, psychic distance; all these pervade both the thought patterns and the unconscious content of every human mind. Scratch a modern person and a "primitive man" shows through. push a chain of scientific reason far enough and magic shines forth. We are ourselves all that has gone before us and to realize the course and continuity of human history we need only to look within ourselves.

# CHAPTER II

# AN ANALYSIS OF THE PRESENT SITUATION

## A Period Like the Renaissance

Donald Nugent of the University of Kentucky has demonstrated
that the interest in occultism today is very like the interest in witchcraft and the occult in the period of the Renaissance.[1] He observes
that the degree of interest in magic that characterized the period
of the revival of learning is also true of our day. Nugent cites Theo-
dore Roszak as also giving evidence of the integral part that occultism
plays in the modern counter culture. In a way similar to that of
Dr. Pattison, the psychiatrist; Donald Nugent, the historian, points
out that both the Renaissance and our own day are transitional peri-
ods.[2] Additionally, Nugent points to the increase of anti-intellectual-
ism and the attack on conventional learning (of which even Marshall
McLuhan's criticism was a apart) as a prelude to the revival of the
occult.

Nugent's interesting essay quotes a number of authorities to the
effect that witchcraft is more widespread today than at any time
since the Renaissance. While declaring that his statistics are unreliable, Nugent gives us an estimate of 60,000 sorcerers in France,
30,000 witches in England, and after only five years' growth, 20,000
Satanists in the United States.[3]

## Movies, Television and Books

Only someone who has been away from the United States for a number
of years would need documentation of the fact that the occult is
very much a part of our daily life. The bookstands are literally
full of books, hard cover and paperback, dealing with one aspect
or the other of the occult. Besides my own book, RELIGION IN
THE AGE OF AQUARIUS, which sought to give evidence of this

widespread interest, we might also mention a number of other recent books that document the fascinations of occultism in an introductory fashion.

Nat Freeland has given us an introduction to THE OCCULT EXPLOSION.[4] Peter Rowley has written of his informal study of the new religions of American youth in NEW GODS IN AMERICA.[5] Hal Lindsey, the conservative theological writer, has given us a shrill warning against all forms of occultism in SATAN IS ALIVE AND WELL ON PLANET EARTH.[6] Anyone interested in the size of this phenomenon would do well to stop at the nearest bookstore and browse for awhile.

On the broader literary field we need not be experts to notice the occult theme that plays such a large role in our most popular literature. The best selling Gothic novel, GREEN DARKNESS by Anya Seton,[7] revolves around reincarnation presented as a fact. the heroine finds herself slipping basck into the past because of an unresolved crime. Within a few weeks of each other two publishers brought out books concerning vampires, Leonard Wolf's A DREAM OF DRACULA,[8] and Raymond McNally and Radu Florescu's IN SEARCH OF DRACULA.[9] Among novels we have had THE EXORCIST[10] and THE OTHER,[11] both chilling tales of the supernatural that take the occult as fact. In the realm of anthropology there have been few books as well received as those of Carlos Castaneda, who records his journey from membership in the scientific community to membership in the brotherhood of sorcerers. His books include THE TEACHINGS OF DON JUAN,[12] A SEPARATE REALITY,[13] and JOURNEY TO IXTLAN.[14]

The best selling book of many seasons has been JONATHAN LIVINGSTON SEAGULL by Richard Bach,[15] which is an occultic classic. Bach has worked together the idea of Karma with other Indian and some Christian elements to produce a philosophical nail-soup that has caught the public's attention in a way that few books ever do.

It is important to note that few people sense the discontinuity of the philosophical ideas involved in JONATHAN LIVINGSTON SEAGULL. Most people seem to feel that it is quite consonant with their Christian faith. Apparently only the most conservative church members take doctrine seriously enough to become upset over the ideas put forth by Bach.

The list of movies with occultic themes is extensive, including "Baron Blood," "Blacula," "Captain Sinbad," "Countess Dracula," "Daughters of Satan," "Dracula, A.D. 1972," and "Vampire Circus." But none of these movies measure up to the witchcraft themes of several made-for-television movies. Again, none of them is as strikingly made as "Rosemary's Baby." The one that comes closest to "Rosemary's Baby" is "The Possession of Joel Delaney."

Occultism turns up in our books and play, not only in the traditional way of witchcraft and curses and spells, but increasingly today in the guise of science or science fiction. We might note three general areas in which the occult appears in at least a pseudo-scientific way; one, in connection with space travel, U.F.O.'s and other astral phenomena; two, in connection with studies of primitive peoples such as Castaneda's investigation of Don Jaun; and three, in connection with psychosomatic medicine, faith healing and E.S.P.

Of course, all books dealing with space travel, primitive people and faith healing, not to mention E.S.P., are not approached from an occultic angle. However, a very large number of the most popular books in these areas are. The immediate connection to E.S.P. and faith healing is evident. Occultic writers welcome the chance to find even the most tenuous support for the existence of paranormal forces. In connection with anthropological studies, the outstanding examples are the writings of Carlos Castaneda concerning Indian sorcery. The area of science fiction has long lent itself to occultic topics. The U.F.O. interest fits in perfectly with sectarian religious and occultic interest. Undoubtedly the most well developed melding of science, science-fiction and off-beat religion is the work of Erich Von Daniken in GODS FROM OUTER SPACE[16] and CHARIOTS OF THE GODS.[17]

Van Daniken's major thesis is that the mythology of the Old and New Testaments is based upon actual observances of extraterrestrial visitors in space ships. Put bluntly, he wants us to believe that God is an astronaut and that the story of Christ coming down to earth and ascending into heaven is a garbled version of primitive men sighting people in space ships. Von Daniken marshalled many interesting facts about ancient archaeology and mythology to prove his case. The fact that he jumps all over history as well as all over the map makes us less credulous than might otherwise be the case. It is safe to say the Von Daniken attaches much of his argument to the famous U.F.O. scare of a few years ago. He builds on the widespread greeting of the U.F.O.'s as religious epiphanies and carries this line of occultic thinking to its logical conclusion.

## The Occult in the Seventies and Eighties

The widespread interest in occultism today is not debatable. Occultism pervades every area of American life. One issue of PLAYBOY magazine contained a small booklet as an insert advertising whiskeys which shows each drink associated with a different sign of the zodiac.[18]  Zodiac signs decorate all manner of clothing and are formed into all kinds of jewelry for every age group. However, I would rather turn to exploring experiences of people with occultism instead of illustrating the obvious.

On Monday through Wednesday, November 5-7, 1984, seven college coeds gathered around a homemade ouija board to play a game they called "Teacup", a sort of ouija. They were amazed when "a spirit" took control of the cup and spelled out a story of incest and murder. The more information they received, the more curious but also frightened they became. Soon other groups of students began to play the game. The "spirit" gave his name, which checked out as a real family in the locality. Even more frightened, the group came to see me. I tried to discourage them, but they were so curious, some of them continued the "game." In several interviews I urged the students to give up "Teacup" and suggested that they ask the Campus Catholic Chaplain to bless their dorm and ask God to exorcise any evil spirits. Both the students and the priest agreed to do this.

One interesting note, this happened just before final examinations in the fall term. I have been consulted by coeds who got involved with seances at precisely this time of the school year on at least three other campuses. One wonders if the magnet for such activity is Halloween or the anxiety over finals.

The following brief cases were recorded after a coffee hour held in my honor at a mid-western college. I wrote down my impressions of what was said by the people there immediately after the event.

The young lady is blonde, around 23, married. She volunteers her experiences with E.S.P. The meeting is a small group of faculty, students and townspeople who have gathered after a lecture to discuss the occult. She identifies herself as an identical twin. Her sister lives in Denver, two thousand miles away. She reports that they do not write each other often and when, in concern, she starts to pick up the phone to call her, the phone always rings first and it is her sister calling her. Upon questioning as to whether she hears her sister's voice in her mind, she answers, "All the time."

Looking around the room, we see a lady in her early thirties. She has an extremely interested look on her face and keeps glancing at her husband. She identifies herself as of Catholic background, but not very much up on religious matters or concerns. She expresses her amazement at the sort of things talked about in the lecture and at this gathering. Then she asks, "What about dreams?" When told dreams are important she volunteers: "Once, before any of my three children were born, I dreamed several times that I saw my second daughter, my third child, clearly as a grown child. It was her, there is no mistake about it." She then turns to her husband and asked, "But you've had some dreams, too. Don't you want to tell them about them?" But he didn't trust the group as much as his wife did, and we didn't learn his story.

The connection of religion, healing and the occult is very real, although the basic underlying structures and belief systems of theology, medicine (especially psychotherapy) and occult wisdom are blurred in the twentieth century. The New Testament is full of stories of Jesus casting out demons and healing the sick. There are seventy-one instances of the terms "demon", "demoniac," "demoniacs," "demonic" and "demons" in the New Testament alone, according to the COMPLETE CONCORDANCE TO THE REVISED STANDARD VERSION BIBLE.[19] Additionally, the term "devil" occurs thirty-four times in the New Testament, and the word "devilish" once. The term "healing" is used, with reference to Jesus four times, and Acts 9:34 says "Aeneas, Jesus Christ heals you. . ."

The Old Testament also contains much material that shows the interrelations (and conflicts) between occultism, religion and healing. Saul and the witch of Endor, Moses and the magicians of Pharoah, and Baalam and his unsuccessful attempt to curse the Israelites (Numbs. 22: 21-33).

Outside the Bible record, we know that people have gone to witches to have sexual problems cured and fertility made possible all through history. Today African witch doctors and psychiatrists work together with native patients. Witch women in the deep South cure warts. Television personalities consult astrologers for aid with their problems.

23

Cases of exorcism of demons by Anglican and Roman Catholic priests as well as by Protestant ministers are on the rise.

The following case, reported by a psychiatrist who is an active Presbyterian layman is certainly not strange in our era.

## Mary

"Here is one case history, involving astrology. Mary, age 27, came to see me 'because my husband made me.' And when I asked her why he made her, she responded, "He thinks I'm nervous and he wants me to shape up -- I may be nervous, but I'm not going to change my life style.' After a pause, she added, 'He thinks I nag him -- we may nag each other.' "Over a period of three interviews, she gave me the following significant history. Her mother and father separated when she was five years of age. Mary blamed her nagging mother. She said, however, that although she did not remember her father too well, she was aware that she didn't like him. There were no siblings. the mother worked, leaving the sickly grandmother to care for Mary. Mary did not like her grandmother. The mother did not attend church, but made Mary take part in church plays and choirs, although she never went to Sunday school. She hated the activities her mother made her attend. As Mary grew up her mother got her to 'everything -- Scouts, school, clubs, dancing lessons, etc.' Her mother took her 'everywhere -- to all good things, like ballets, operas, plays, and made me aware of the great sacrifices in order to buy the many tickets.' Her mother's chief interest at home was caring for dozens of cats she collected and raised. The grandmother eventually died, after a long illness. Mary did not care at all. Things did not get any better, however. Finally Mary got through high school and went to another city to college -- glad to get away from home. But because of financial conditions, Mary could not return for the sophomore year. She got a job and lived at home. During the year she met a young man, and after a whirlwind courtship, they married in two months. 'Not giving Mother time to get her claws into me to hold onto me.' The mother abominated the husband. She calmed down, continued working, and more or less left them alone. The marriage went all right for awhile. Then Mary began to annoy her husband by doing such things as sleeping until noon -- after having read all night, letting in stray cats and dogs, and never having dinner until nine or ten at night. She argued that that's the way they always did things at home, because 'Mother hated the kitchen and always had trouble getting a meal on the table.'

She added that mother was a poor sleeper, too. Mary then said, 'My mother was terrible, but I supposed she did all she could for me.'

Mary's husband got tired of this type of living and begged his wife to 'come to and shape up.' 'Nothing doing,' she said. After several years of arguing about 'how we live' the husband insisted that she see a psychiatrist. The patient would not discuss her father and was even reluctant to give the above history, but when I asked her if she would agree that her life style was patterned after her mother's, she promptly and loudly denied being like her mother at all. After the third visit the left the office saying, 'I don't need help, my husband does.' The couple moved to another city and I did not hear from her for seventeen months. then one day she was visiting home and called for an appointment. She said that she had just wanted to tell me that things are going better. She volunteered the following statement: "Doctor, I found out that part of my trouble was hating my mother and I guess, to deny this I tried to be like her. You might say that I was tied to her apron strings -- but not really -- you see, my hate turned to pity and at this point I sent mother all kinds of gifts. Then I began to understand why mother is such a despicable person.' I interupted her to ask how she came to know these things. She answered, 'Doctor, do you believe in astrology? Carl Jung did. You probably know. After we moved I met some girls who invited me to their astrology class. They had a Ph.D. teacher, like Jung, who had also written his dissertation on some astrological subject. We had lessons every week and I got a new lease on life.' I asked her then, how? And she answered, 'Well, I first learned a lot about myself. First, I am a Capricorn, an earth sign and I don't like the earth sign. I really found out that I was like that goat out on the mountainside. Cold, self-seeking and determined. You know, don't you, the characteristics of the various sun signs?' I admitted that I didn't know very much about astrology and she continued, 'My moon is in Virgo, another damn earth sign.' Then Mary described her solar chart, giving the locations of all her planets, their aspects and so forth. She continued, 'Say, doctor, you'd like to hear this. My chart showed exactly how I hate my mother. She was living her life through me and I wasn't allowed to be myself. I had to do what Mother had always wanted to do. How about that?'

"Did you get around to the working out of your mother's horoscope?" I asked.

'Now, that's where I really found out some important things,' she

25

answered. 'Mother is a Scorpio, with Leo rising and she has the worse characteristics of both.' Mary then explained to me why she now understands why her mother is the way she is and she also blames 'that grandmother,' who, it turns out, hated Mary's mother and blamed God for taking her other daughter. Mary told how her grandmother 'took to the bed' after her favorite child's death and never got up except to 'bustle and fuss around about me.' Mary added that grandmother would never let play mud-pies, or otherwise get dirty, and she likely noted the irony of her being so mixed up in earth signs.

I asked Mary about her father's chart. She said that she had not done one, as she does not know the exact time of his birth. It is interesting to note that Mary was reluctant to talk about her husband and would not discuss her father at all. At this point she showed interesting anxiety, said that she had taken up enough of my time, and that she had to go. I asked her to tell me briefly, before she left, how she and her husband were getting along. She said, 'Much better' and added, 'He's a Leo, with a Leo rising. He's king of the beasts. He's like that short story I read in Freshmen English, a cock-less crow, so I let him.' As she got to the door to leave, she shook hands and told me that she thought I would make a good astrologer!

"Now, a comment to this effect -- I would say that astrology had definitely helped Mary. First, by giving her a nomenclature by which she could think about the characteristics of her personality and then by giving her some understanding of herself, her mother and her husband. All of which resulted in lessening her anxiety and tension. Her neuroses is still there, however, but she is more comfortable with it. Also she has found new friends, new interests and an increased zest for life."[20]

**Why People May Turn to the Occult**

Our panoramic display of the present widespread interest in occultic practices suggest several things to me. First, there is a residual mythological element in every mind, in every time, including our own. Secondly, there is an apparent inability on the part of many people today to relate to clergymen and the organized church for assistance with their problems. Thirdly, the inability to relate to the church is now being parallelled with an inability to relate to psychiatrists and psychologists. Fourthly, it is definitely possible, as the above case history demonstrates, that there are psychothera-peutic uses of occultic materials, suggesting that astrology may be one way of finding out who we are.

This last point about the self-treatment that some people may be able to give themselves through occultic practices, may tie in with a deeper fact about human nature, that men and women often want to help themselves. The surge of do-it-yourself and self-improvement projects that gather so much interest in America suggest to me that just as people may take courses on how to learn to have self-confidence or how to speak in public, may also mean people buy occultic books in order to get to know themselves. All of us have problems we wish to solve by ourselves in a way that takes account of the breadth and mystery of the human personality more than is generally the case in professional counseling.

Such a thrust would fit in well with the tenets of the most recent variety of counter cultural philosophy that I call the way of the plain person and that Daniel Yankelovich calls the new naturalism.[21] One of these tenets according to Yankelovich is: "To de-emphasize aspects of nature illuminated by science; instead, to celebrate all the unknown, the mystical, and the mysterious elements of nature."[22] Another of these tenets is: "To devalue detachment, objectivity, and noninvolvement as methods for finding truth; to arrive at truth instead, by direct experience, participation, and involvement."[23]

We need to be aware of the fact that what is considered occultic by many of us in the church or in psychology was not always considered so different from the regular content of religion and of the philosophical attempt to understand man. St. Thomas Aquinas believed in astrology, attributing the effects of the stars on man to "celestial impressions on man,"[24] as well as basing his belief on the philosophy of Aristotle.[25] The theologians and philosophers of the middle ages certainly believed in the reality of witchcraft as did Luther, Calvin and the other Reformers and, as we all know, the Puritan Divines certainly did, also. In our own day, inerestingly enough, ultra conservative Protestant theologians believe in the reality of demons and spirit-possession as is shown by Hal Lindsey's book, SATAN IS ALIVE AND WELL ON PLANET EARTH.[26]

While I am not sure that it is any too healthy to attribute the reality that Lindsey does to evil spirits, it is nevertheless a paradox that while clergymen are better prepared to help people with their problems today, their exposure to psychological techniques may have made them less acceptable to this mystical generation than the literalistic and moralistic fundamentalists who have no doubt about the factuality of spiritual phenomena. Whatever the theological background of the clergyman, it is clear that the children of the new naturalism are not sympathetic with the clinical training and orientation of either the clergy or the psychologists. Only people who are sensitive to the expression of deep feelings, the anxiety, seeking and desire for mystery, to what young people call the "vibrations" of people, are able to help men and women in our time.

The following case, written up by a young person herself, illustrates the searching sensitivity of this generation:

### An Occult Commune Based on Science Fiction[27]

"The individuals who made of the Botherhood, and I call them individuals for the Brotherhood, never tried to give anyone any more importance other than that of an individual, came together because they were failures by society's standards. Their views on life, their beliefs, were being squashed by society and they were alone.

"The Brotherhood was formed in a small town in eastern Kentucky. In large cities the strain of society is prevalent but in a small community of 1400 the strain is concentrated. It started with two young men, one was fifteen and the other eighteen. Freddie, the fifteen year old, was starting, even at this young age, to become bored with life. The small town offered no real recreation and so he spent his spare time reading and through his reading his life style was formed. Unfortunately, it was not accepted in the small town. Because of this parents did not allow their children to associate with him, but that really wasn't much of a problem for the parents since very few people wanted to become friends with an out-of-place individual. And so Freddie was alone. He believed strongly in his views on life but had no one to share them with, so he turned to drinking -- at the age of fifteen.

"Michael was the individual to first start the Brotherhood. His parents were strict Catholics and Michael was raised as such, being an altar boy when he was young. When Michael was twelve his parents divorced and his mother remarried. Michael was sent to live with his grandparents. The emotional strain he went through at this time was overpowering and he had to be sent to a psychiatrist. When knowledge of this escaped into the community Michael was continually ridiculed by his peers. Fights broke out often and Michael lost most of them, so he took up Karate and became a second degree black belt. He started winning fights but he felt guilty about winning. He became confused and so he decided to study for the priesthood.

"After a time he realized that what he was studying did not make sense for him and so he dropped his studies, becoming more confused with life. He took up reading and through reading and traveling reformed his life style. This life style was not accepted in the small community and so he was alone.

"I was never told how Freddie and Michael met but it is easy to see how two outcasts in such a small community could get together. It seems that through their heavy reading they had both read STRANGER IN A STRANGE LAND by Robert A. Heinlein.[28] The idea of such a brotherhood that is found in the book appealed to both of them. The closeness, the sharing that was in the Water Brothers was something they both wanted and so the Brotherhood was formed.

"At first the book was taken literally. In the Water Brothers communal living was stressed and when Bernie, a twenty-five year old woman was allowed to 'share water,' this was started, to a certain degree. But after a while Freddie and Michael could see that being ruled by a book was just as bad as being ruled by society and so they started out to re-evaluate their brotherhood."

When men and women feel lost, they will seek out anything that promises them help in finding themselves. I think that is what the cases of the woman who turned to astrology and the coed who turned to a Brotherhood based on a work of science fiction proves. Just what these people found in these unlikely spiritual sources is the topic of the next chapter.

# CHAPTER III

## SELF-THERAPY: THEOLOGY AND PSYCHOLOGY

### The Basic Tenets of Occultism: Sympathy

The belief-structure of occultism seems very complex on the surface but underneath it is comparatively simple. This can be illustrated by analysis of the beliefs of the Brotherhood:

"In order to join the Brotherhood you must first read the book, STRANGER IN A STRANGE LAND. After a time, when you have talked to the other individuals about the basic regulations, ideas, and such that make up the Brotherhood you are allowed to share water.

"Up to this time you are a 'brother in essence' which means you are a brother without having been brought officially into the group. The 'brother in essence' must be told of certain things and during the ceremony, which Michael usually performs, everything which the Brotherhood is based upon is summarized so that the brother will be sure of his decision, before he shares water. After sharing water the person is now a part of the Brotherhood.

"The ceremonial initiation speech will be presented in the following paragraphs. It usually takes place in a cemetery, but this is not necessary. A cemetery was usually chosen because of its solitude and quietness and infrequent visitors. In this rural community many of the inhabitants were familiar with ghost stories and did not wish to be in the vicinity of the cemetery at night.

"Thou art God, My Brother, as is a blade of grass, a tree, a cloud or a breeze, for it has been said that God cannot help but note a sparrow who falls from the sky for the sparrow is God. Hold this true, worship all things for through this worship you will learn to grow and have true understanding of all things."

"In my hand is a goblet of water. In a very few moments, I shall hand this goblet to you and if you decide to join the Brotherhood you shall drink, pledging that you are dedicated to the purpose of becoming a whole person. You know of our teachings, that we stress several things and before you drink this life-giving water I shall explain them to you. Then you shall be sure of yourself at the time when only a right decision must be made."

"You must hold true to the three words the brotherhood is based upon -- Love, Honesty and Trust. There must be a total and never faulting belief in these three words. You must at all times be totally honest, no matter what the consequences. In time you will find you will become totally honest with all the world and this will bring you closer to perfection. You must at all times trust totally, no matter what the consequences seem to be, so that in time you will learn to trust all of the world and therefore bring yourself closer to perfection. You must be ready to lay your life, your being, in the palms of another brother's hands and feel absolutely safe. You will find that after you have reached this point that love will come naturally, perhaps in many different forms. When it does come you will be able to love everyone and this will bring you closer to being a whole person, a perfect person."

"Yet after you have gone this far you are not perfect, for there is still another major step you must take. You must, no matter what the consequences, do what you truly believe is right for you. Many times this may appear to be hurtful to others, but it will always come out glorious in the end for inner peace has been obtained."

"You recognize that your life is your own, you are a free person and that when you drink this water you are pledging to us with total honesty and trust that you are going to live your life in search of perfection. Then, because you are an individual, we do not control your behavior, but when we see that your are destroying yourself and failing to grow we will take action if you are violating your pledge to the Brotherhood."

"You know that whatever you do in your lifetime will be supported by the Brotherhood, even if some of the brothers do not understand your actions. You will always be forgiven for your wrong doings if you set them straight yourself, or call on your brothers to help you."

"We do not hurry, we have great patience which we have obtained by trying to perfect ourselves. If your are committing a wrongness then we will give you all the time you need to correct it, if we feel you are truly trying to correct it. Again I remind you of some of our brothers who have progressed enough to establish truthfulness."

"You do not have to progress in the other brothers' footsteps for we are all different with different goals and ideas. We are only a brotherhood because of our basic drive in life -- to become perfect."

"Most of us believe that anything can be done when enough concentration is applied but it takes a great deal of discipline to achieve certain goals. You must first learn to be humble and to be tolerant of others, for with such power you could unconsciously destroy the world and yourself."[1]

## Occult Theological Principles

We will not attempt to trace the theology of occultism historically, for that would take several volumes. Rather, we here will briefly digest the theological ideas that underlie all occultic thought, past and present. The similarity of some of these principles to certain debased forms of Christian theology should be noted.

**Dualism:** All forms of occultic thought, from full-blown witchcraft to the casting of horoscopes believes in theological dualism. Dualism assumes that the world is a great battleground between ultimate, basic forces of good and evil. An historical example of dualism was Manichaeism, the heretical version of Christianity that seduced Augustine in his earlier years. Manichaeism firmly believed in the existence of two gods, the one good and the other evil. Earlier in Christian history, Marcion had introduced dualism into Christian thought by declaring the God of the New Testament (the Father of Jesus Christ) to be good, and the god of the Old Testament, evil. Dennis Wheatley in his book, THE DEVIL AND ALL HIS WORKS, echoes this dualism, saying: "Existence as we know it is dominated by two powers -- Light and Darkness."[2]

The following report demonstrates the attraction of darkness for some:

## The Setting and Decor of the Occult

Imagine yourself walking down a major street of a medium-sized city with fewer than one hundred thousand residents. A small, very well known liberal arts college lies on your left; to the right opens a sedate residential street. You turn right and walk under the graceful old trees that line the sidewalk. On the right is a brick bungalow, the home of a nationally known psychiatrist. Just down the way, the chairman of a department of a major university makes his home. Hardly the place to go witch-hunting? Hardly, and yet across the street, one house down, is the location of a coven. Five people -- three men, two women -- and all of them witches.

We cross the street and climb the stairs of an old mansion whose air is one of tiredness. It is not a run-down building. The house is painted and swept, but its glory is gone. Now it is divided into apartments, two up and two down. We go upstairs and knock at a door. It opens at our rap, of its own weight. The door is not locked, nor has it a lock at all. The rooms of the coven stand open to the world.

What rooms these are! There are five rooms, all differently decorated. In the room we enter, dolls, painted and distorted and torn, are hanging everywhere. A crushed skull stands on a shelf. A coffee table supports a birdcage in the middle of the room. Inside the cage is a painted doll rather than a bird. From time to time someone takes a sword and "torments" the doll, all the while calling it "Cosmic Charlie".

One corner contains a fireplace. A gas-log is burning there. Several other persons are seated in front of this fire, "grooving" or "flashing" on the flickering gas light -- for the people in this room are almost completely "stoned," or intoxicated on drugs.

Someone greets us and hands us the skull. This is a grotesque item, old, brown, with the jaw missing and with a crushed-in line running from the right eye to the top of the skull. The boy who has given us the skull tells us that it is the remains of a murder victim, dug up in an adjoining city by black cultic friends who sent it on to them as a present. We are offered a pot cigarette, decline it, and wander to another room.

Walking through the crowd of guests in the dim light, we are struck by the wild expressions on the faces of some of the people present. A tall, beautiful, black-haired girl sways back and forth as if hypnotized. Incidentally, some of the guests are rather distantly "tripped out" on LSD.

The next room is brightly painted and at first reminds us of a little girl's room. There is one significant difference -- all the furniture in this room has been very carefully bolted to the ceiling. Brightly glowing, hip colors cover the table, four chairs, dishes, silverware, glasses, and flowers that hang suspended from the ceiling. This witty, amusingly decorated room lightens our outlook, and some of the sense of evil that we felt in the other room falls away from us.

The next room returns some of that foreboding, because of its color as well as on account of the direction in which it drives our thoughts. It is a small room, painted completely black; a deep, ebony, shining black, from floor to ceiling. Only one object is in the room, a brass bed; all of it is painted black too, except for the large rails at the head and foot, which glow richly in the light falling from the next room. There are no lights and no other objects in the "bedroom."

We walk back toward the front room and become aware of exotic music coming from a record player hidden somewhere in a dark corner. A few of the people in the larger room are moving back and forth to the music, dancing or "grooving" to the weird sounds. From their behavior, we would judge that at least some of these people are homosexuals.

Among the things mentioned by the people at this party was their connection with other black occult groups in neighboring cities. The characteristics of the cult members seemed to be the following: All of them are young, under thirty for the most part, with high school and some college education. Almost all are now out of college or high school and working at white-collar jobs. All seem to be single, but many are living together, often with several men and women sharing the same apartment. The use of wine, beer, marijuana, and drugs, as well as psychedelics, seems to be universal among them. While totally alienated from the society in which they are located, they seem to be apolitical. Each person seems turned in upon himself or herself, fascinated by the internal contradictions he finds within himself. Their philosophy of life is best described as a sensationalist hedonism. For them, evil is more fun than good, and a great pleasure is derived from shocking and frightening the more passive types of "cool" students who live in other apartments in their area. One such very upset student who visited the coven says he believes they would like to make a human sacrifice, just to see what that trip would be like.

In occultism there are many choices, but they are contained within this overall dualaism and fall into two "paths", the path of Light (good) and the path of Darkness (evil). The vast range of choice's open to the person who feels the world is open, with room for human freedom, is foregone by the occultist. The only choice the occultist really makes is the evaluation of the chances for victory of the two contending forces. Most people in history have felt that good would eventually triumph, so they have chosen the "white" path, but a significant minority have felt that evil might win, and thus have become "black" or evil witches.

A very large amount of fundamentalist theology, with its emphasis upon a personal devil, belief in demon-possession, faith healing, etc., is close to occultism. The "fire and brimstone" type of revivalist preaching comes close to the dualism -- or Manichaeism -- of putting Satan in constant warfare against God.

## Sympathy

Second only to the basic dualism of occult theology is the functional doctrine of sympathy, or sympathetic magic. This view is based on a very ancient idea that "like influences like." We see this in a multitude of ways in religion, various forms of magic, and auto-suggestion and hypnosis. The earliest recollection I have of this doctrine of sympathy goes back to the Negro lady who cared for me as a child in Charleston, South Carolina. Her treatment for warts was straight out of voodoo, for it consisted of cutting off a potato peeling, putting it on the wart and then burying it in the ground. The idea was that when the potato peeling rotted and dis-appeared, the wart would, too. This perfectly expressed the doctrine of sympathy, of like producing like. Much more famous examples that are know to us from books and plays involve the making of voodoo dolls of the intended victim. The idea here is that anything that is done to the doll will also be done to the person, since the doll is like the person and the doll has an affinity with the person through the parts of his body that are incorporated in it.

Sympathy operates in a more purified form, in many religious practices that we think little about. An example might be the attitude of prayer. We kneel to pray in order to show reverence and humility but of course one may remain irreverent and unhumble even on his knees. At other times we raise our eyes towards heaven and perhaps place our hands together in a steeple-like position with the hands pointed sky-ward in order to illustrate the attitude of aspiration toward the Divine. Of course, such a position may genuinely express our state or it may not, but we are taught to adopt such gestures and positions in religion becasue of the large element of sympathy that is residual even in modern religion and is central to occultism even in our time.

The concept of sympathy or sympathetic magic underlies the whole conception of astrology with its idea of the twelve cardinal signs of the Zodiac that ascribe certain characteristics to people because of the supposed characteristics of the planet that rules their birthdate. For example, since the planet Mars is associated with mythology, Mars is said to be war-like, exhibiting aggressiveness and boldness. On the basis of this sympathetic relationship a person born under the sign of Aries, ruled by Mars, is said to be aggressive, bold, a leader and a pioneer. On what evidence? Only on the evidence of some supposed vibrations or sympathy between the planets and the individual born in that part of the year said to be dominated by this planet. If we look further we will find that the planet Mars was named Mars becasue it seems to be reddish in color and red is associated with war and bloodshed. Thus sympathy rules all in this kind of thinking.

We could illustrate the doctrine of sympathy in each of the so-called occult sciences as well as in many areas of investigation that have become more respectable in recent years. At one time serious professors believed in phrenology, the science of the study of the bumps on the head. the great philosopher Hegel even incorporated a section on phrenology in his work, THE PHENOMENOLOGY OF MIND.[3]

It is hard to credit the faith that many nineteenth century people had in the view that the bumps on the outside of the skull could take on the character of the person on the inside of that skull. An underlying acceptance of the doctrine of sympathy was the only reason phrenology could be taken seriously.

Two illustrations of so-called occultic phenomena may sharpen our appreciation of sympathy as a widespread and widely accepted philosophical principle even today. The first consists of a creepy story told about a tombstone in a cemetery in Carey, Ohio. It seems this particular tombstone on the grave of a lady showed an unusual pattern in the stone on the reverse of the tombstone. it was a raised spot shaped like a teardrop. The story that circulated about this stone was that the lady had feared that her husband might kill her and told some of her friends that if he did succeed in doing this and was undetected, then a teardrop would form on her tombstone. The stone did show this feature and was changed. According to the story, a similar teardrop appeared on the second stone as well. This is a good example of sympathy, even if the entire story was made up as an explanation of an unusual configuration in the stone of a grave marker that had no particular murderous history.

Almost all horror stories and other scary tales turn on the sympathetic idea. Perhaps the most famous is Edgar Allen Poe's story of THE TELL-TALE HEART. Poe lets us see a man whose conscience is burdened by guilt that mistakes every rhythmic thumping sound for the beating of the heart of his victim.

The very same source that told me about the weeping tombstone also told me of the ghostly noise in a Chicago street. According to this story, a young girl returned to her home which faced on a side street, and found robbers murdering her family. She ran out of the house for help and in her terror went right into the street, striking the side of a passing car, which killed her. Now, according to my informant, as cars pass this house, you can hear a thump hit the side of the car although nothing can be seen. In late 1979, I was told a quite similar story by parishioners who abandoned a "haunted" house in the Ohio countryside and moved to a trailer in a nearby town.

The conception of sympathy plays a role also in graphology, or handwriting analysis. This study, which has become respectable in recent years, declares that there is a connection between the size and shape of the letters we write and our inner character traits. It probably has as much foundation as a good many other psychological explanations of human behavior.

The social order is often disturbed by the widespread belief in sympathy when people are attacked on the basis of guilt by association. Jesus, of course, was criticized by his contemporaries for associating with men and women of bad moral character. He was said to have a bad character too, since, as the proverb has it, "birds of a feather flock together." This is guilt by association and it is based on sympathetic magic.

**Sympathy as a Means of Coming to Grips with the World:**

Probably most primitive religious ideas and the entire intellectual structure of occultism can be explained by the principles of dualism and sympathy that we have discussed thus far. I give here only a brief outline of some of the major doctrines and practices of religions around the world that are crystalized in occultic beliefs.

Cannibalism has been practiced by human groups since the dawn of time. Apparently the underlying idea is that the qualities of the person whose organs are consumed become part of the person engaging in the rite. Throughout the history of occultism, along the left hand or black magic path, cannibalism or its close cognate, ritual murder, have been practiced. This is mentioned by Dennis Wheatley[4] and Maurice Bessy.[5] The idea behind human sacrifice, and the later practice of animal sacrifice, is that the life of the slain person or beast is in tune with the life of the slayer and consequently will be accepted by the divine power in the place of the one making the sacrifice. The movement from human to animal sacrifice is discernible in the Old Testament text itself (Genesis 22).

The idea of sympathy between the one who makes the sacrifice and the life that is offered up may become sacramentalized as in the case of the scapegoat or the sin offering laid down in the Old Testament. For the Christian, this principle is most clearly seen in the Last Supper and in the sacrament of the Holy Communion based upon it. (Mark 14:17-26, Matthew 26:20-29, Luke 22:14-20 and I Corinthians 11:23-26).

**Imitation:**

Most of the primitive religions, including the tribal religions of the day, and the folk religions of the people of Israel in Old Testament times, contained an element of sympathetic magic that we call fertility rites. These rites, which figure in the book of Hosea, involved the practice of public sexual relations which were felt to stimulate the powers of nature in order to insure good harvest and many lambs. Mircea Eliade[6] reports that such rituals continued in Europe among the peasants of Rumania until the time of his own youth in this country. Such a belief assumes a sympathy between the life of man and the life of the total universe. They also involve, as do the rite of sacrifice, **a doctrine of imitation,** which implies that the broad powers of nature, whether of evil or of good , will imitate the actions of men involved in sacred rituals. This belief surely underlies much of the mumbo-jumbo of magic and of occultic rites as well as much of the content of debased forms of religion.

**Mana:**

The ideas of dualism, sympathy and imitation are all involved in a concept that Mircea Eliade and other historians of religion tell us is central to most primitive religious ideas -- that of **Mana.**[7] The concept of Mana is often called animism, meaning the belief that all of nature is alive; filled with spirit. Interestingly enough these spirits may be good or evil, depending upon human experiences with them.

The most ancient drawings left in the caves of France show hunters disguised as animals. Ancient men mimicked the animals they hunted, believing that by so doing they assimilated their strength and gained them power to conquer them. These animistic views, expressed in imitation, shows the strength of the idea of sympathy, a belief in an attraction between human beings and other beings because of the existence of some universal force binding them together. If this universal force is seen as Mana, then the core ideas of primitive religions and occultism are neatly tied together.

**Vibrations:**

The counter culture of recent years has gone far towards recapturing for itself the most basic ideas of ancient religions and by virture of that, of occultism, as well. We hear much about vibrations in the music that holds the attention of our youth, a concept which the passionate rythms of the electric guitar make easier to feel if not to understand. Vibrations are spoken of as if they were readily apparent to everyone, whereas without the benefit of information from the history of religions, or a knowledge of occultic beliefs, they are well nigh impossible to understand.

Let us theorize that vibrations or "vibes" are modern ways of speaking about the dualism that views the world as a place of contention between the powers of good and evil and the doctrine of sympathy that believes like causes like, since everything is tied together in a living whole. Vibrations, then, represent a central feature of occultism in the midst of the counter culture. Perhaps those who have taken drugs and experienced distorted forms of consciousness find it easy to credit the existence of such a sympathetic force on the basis of their far-out experiences. This may also explain some of the elements that Daniel Yankelovich tells us are present in "the new naturalism".[8] Yankelovich is surely right in listing the elements that make up the most recent movement in the counter culture, some of which are:

To emphasize the inner dependence of all things and species in nature.

To place sensory experience ahead of conceptual knowledge.

To de-emphasize science and to celebrate the unknown, the mystical and the mysterious elements of nature.

to express oneself nonverbally; to avoid literary and stylized forms of expression as artificial and unnatural; to rely on exclamations as well as silences, vibrations, and other nonverbal modes of communication.[9]

There are a number of modern attempts to explain "vibrations" and the bond of sympathy which the past several generations have seriously come to believe in.

**Synchronicity:**

Carl Gustav Jung, convinced of the reality of the mystical element in our lives, coined the term -- then the concept of -- synchronicity.[10] By synchronicity, Jung meant to convey an idea put forward long ago by the philosophy of the seventeenth century -- the concept of parallelism. The philosopher Leibnitz spoke of men and things as having monads or soul-atoms,[11] which were private and separate unto themselves. However, although the monads have no windows, there is a universal parallelism, according to Leibnitz, by which the inner activity of each monad is geared and harmonized to the activity of other monads. There is no direct influence of the outer world upon the monad-soul, but nevertheless there is a complete perfection of the inner and outer worlds by virtue of the correlation of all activity through the monad of monads or God. Jung's principle of synchronicity also holds that two events may happen together in time, enriching each other and being perfectly in harmony, without being casually related. Jung did not believe in God, as such, but he did believe in a cosmic dualism in which the evil force is as necessary to and as basic for life as the good force. Over both -- or created through the tension of these two forces -- is the sympathy; the harmony of synchronicity. Leibnitz and Jung both give persuasive arguments for the unity and influence of all things on each other, explaining vibrations, but they do so by appealing to a cosmic determinism. Man's freedom is diminished to the degree that the unified

41

harmony of the universe is enhanced. Man finds himself at home in the world, with his anxieties greatly lessened, but with his range of choices limited, too.

Behaviorism also takes the phenomenon of vibrations seriously, although not because it believes in mysteries. In fact, for behaviorism it is silly to speak of determination of action taking place within a soul or self without influence from the outside. In the behavioristic approach one looks for the unnoticed, unconscious clues that pass at the nonverbal level between people. Body language, the way we carry ourselves, the way we sit, the way we cross our legs, all communicate to others our inner state, by "vibrations", without words.

Body language, nonverbal communication, imitation, all fit in with a role of sympathy, of harmony, and of synchronicity. The pulsing beat of rock music that has the power to mesmerize thousands, also fits into such a vision. The experience of smoking dope or the feeling of good fellowship or an oceanic experience of being "one with the all", also fits in with the occultic worldview. No wonder occult theology is believed in all around us.

**The Journey, the Trip, and the Descent into Hell:**

Some Reformed Christians have found the phrase in the Apostles' Creed and the Nicene Creed, "He descended into Hell," objectionable. This fact only underscores the demythologization, the evacuation of religious content from the "religion" of secularized, modern people. The descent into hell is not only part of the redemptive story of Jesus Christ; it is part of the spiritual history of every human being. Not only Christianity, but Judaism, Hinduism, Islam, Buddhism and the primitive religions all speak of the **descensus ad infernum.**

Occultism -- and the various Eastern religious and eclectic philosophies current in the counter culture -- have one major strength compared to traditional religion in America. All these competitors stress initiation, the rites of passage, including a descent into hell; a journey into the self.

Occultic theology, like the primitive religion of mana or animism from which it springs, holds to the need for the initiatory ritual of death, the descent into hell and the new birth. One may be "born a witch" as Sybil Leek declares[12] but one has to undergo rites to make that inheritance one's own.

The **rites of passage** are educative and evocative of full dedication. Probably the best contemporary account of such an initiation we have is the story of Carlos Castaneda's incorporation into membership in the brotherhood of Mexican sorcerers.[13] The accounts of people who have experienced "trips" on LSD also parallel the traditional accounts of death and rebirth of Siberian and Alaskan Shamans or witchdoctors.

In primitive religion and occultism, the one decision that can be made is the one concerning the power we will serve. Human religiosity is full of "decisions", dedications, convenants, bargains, pleadings, sacrifices, retreats, ashrams, studies and symbolic deaths. In the West, in modern times, these rites of rebirth have been rationalized and intellectualized, even among the revivalistic sects that seem to be growing today. In America and Canada one is manipulated emotionally to make what is, at base, a rationalistic "decision for Christ." The spectrum of religiosity in America is so tightly tied together that the beliefs and techniques of fundamentalistic sects and occultic groups are not so very different, once one discounts the terminology involved. Occultism is very rationalistic and emotion-manipulating, too. but this was not always true of the occult, as the following account of how one becomes a shaman, a magician, shows.

**The Shaman, the Twice-born Man:**

The shaman, often called the medicine man or the witch doctor is a classic example of the twice-born man. While shamanism is a variety of the primitive religions that flourishes in the Arctic regions, we may see the Siberian and Alaskan shaman as a symbol of what is called the medicine man among American Indians, the witchdoctor among tribal Africans, and the holy man among Hindu sects in India. The shaman above all else is a priest, for he represents the people to divine spirits and the spirits to the people.

It is interesting to note how one becomes a shaman. The shaman is not one who is stronger or more intelligent than others, but very often is sickly, of a nervous disposition and sociopathic in his activities. This kind of marginal personality is looked upon by tribal people as one in whom there are cracks or holes through which the spirit world can shine out into the world of everyday.

43

**Dreams:**

The shaman may prove to be one who can heal others simply because he himself is one who has been healed. This healing has to do with the way in which a person becomes known as a shaman, that is through a process of, in Western terms, going insane and returning to some sort of unity of personality. The shaman is a person who dies to self, descends into hell, makes a spirit journey and returns again to his people as a twice-born man. The manner in which this death and descent into hell is carried out is through the dream.

To slip away into dreams, to forget the everyday reality and to major in the innermost symbols that arise from our subconscious is to court schizophrenia from the modern standpoint. However, in the rites of passage that a person who wishes to become a shaman follows, the road into the self is followed so that the person can enter again the dream time of the ancestors of man. To journey to the dream time is to journey to the origins of the world, to the time before time began, to the eternal, which exists always beneath and alongside the world of time. To allow oneself to fall back into the chaos of dream symbols is to return eventually, by way of a transit of the hell of fears and anxieties that lie within to the eternal center where there is peace and personal integration. the shaman-to-be searches for the keys of his own personality. He searches for the inner strength that enables him to live with his nervous disorders and to become an inner-directed person. He looks for a totem, a symbol out of his experience that can serve as a badge of his authority. He looks, in the Hindu and Buddhist traditions, for the mandala. In the Buddhism of northern Asia, he may look for a mantra, a divine sound that will crystalize the meaning of existence for him. He comes back from his journey with a secret word which is the inner-most source of his strength. For St. Paul it was the secret doctrine that Christ is Lord. For the person who follows the Marharishi in Transcendental Meditation today it is a single sound, which gives them peace.

The occultic teacher also seeks this inner knowledge of self, becoming a kind of shaman. Meditation, prayers and the analysis of one's dreams, play a part in becoming a witch or occultic leader. In the modern world one may seek self knowledge through astrology or other occultic practices in order to escape from anxiety or phychological threat.[14] Today the occultist may utilize drugs as part of the exploration of the self. In all events he must wrestle with the spirit, coming to an understanding of spiritual forces that make him different in many respects from the ordinary person.

**Elitism:**

It is said that the Christian church rejected the Neo-Platonic version of the faith because it taught that there were many levels of Christians. Christians were said to differ in the degree of their spirituality according to the knowledge they had of doctrine. This was an example of spiritual elitism that would have broken the body of Christ concept in which each individual was equal and equally necessary to the life of the church. Occultism represents human self-assertiveness and insists upon the need for knowledge and the possibility of becoming superior in wisdom and spirituality. It is fair to say that there is no idea of democracy in occultism. It appears that people enter the study of occult because, in contemporary language, they are on ego trips. This is rather basic occult theology, that only whose who strongly desire to have secret knowledge, will attain it. We note that people who become famous in occultic matters are of a strong personality at least from the point of view of self-assertiveness. Sybil Leek, Aleister Crowley and other witches are not modest people. It is undoubtedly the case that among modern people those who are looking for outlets for a strong individualistic urge might well consider turning to the occult.

The emphasis upon elitism and self-assertion in occultism forms one of its most severe contrasts with Christianity. Christianity in theory, if not in practice, teaches that one should humble himself before God and stresses that in matters of salvation self-assertion can accomplish nothing. The emphasis upon the salvation wrought by Christ and the unmerited grace of God plays havoc with ego-centric spiritual views, although legalistic systems of human works keep cropping up in Christianity.

The world of the occult is a world of will. The fact that it is the human will that must be strengthened and asserted comes up again and again in the literature of witchcraft. The person who would master the occultic techniques must have a strong will unfailingly bent on attaining whatever object is desired. Indeed, all of the rituals, symbols and paraphernalia of occultism are used in order to concentrate the power of the will. Language is used to raise the emotions to a frenzy. Imitative gestures are used to externalize the wishes of the occultist and symbols and other actions act out the intentions of the spell or curse. Obviously, the more dominating the personality of the occultist, the more convincing all this will be to those who are open to occultic influences.

## Reincarnation:

Reincarnation, basically, is a millennia old religious belief in the survival of physical death by human personality. It differs from other doctrines of the immortality of the soul, and from the Christian doctrine of the Resurrection from the dead to eternal life, in that the Reincarnation belief holds that the immortal soul not only survives death but also returns again into the world of history, taking on a new body at each rebirth.

Throughout Asia, particularly India, Ceylon, Thailand, Burma, Turkey, Syria and Lebanon, as well as in the far eastern section of Alaska close to Soviet Asia, many cases of claimed "reincarnations" occur. This is hardly surprising since the great religions of Hinduism, Buddhism and Jainism all teach the reality of Reincarnation as part of their common doctrine of Karma. Karma holds that a person's status in life is determined by his or her actions in previous lives. Karma is considered the cosmic law of moral cause and effect. The soul is considered indestructable in this line of thought but the conditions of the world (hardly good for most Asians at any time) are justified by Karma, thus producing social inertia.

Not only the Hindu and Buddhist religious texts (the Upanishads, the Theravada legends) but the Dialogues of the foundational Western philosopher, Plato, teach the doctrine of Reincarnation. Plato has Socrates speak of the transmigration of the soul in THE APOLOGY, and in THE PHAEDO Socrates specifically rejects the objections to life after death of Simmias and Cebes in this formulation, saying: "For if the soul exists before birth, and in coming to life and being born can be born only from death and dying, must she not after death continue to exist, since she has to be born again?"[15]

Christian theology rejected the Greek doctrine of Reincarnation (which was taught by the Christian theologian, Origen) and, in general, Western philosophy did too. However, throughout Western Christian history, there have been thinkers who held to a belief in Reincarnation, beginning with the Manichaeans and including Bruno, Goethe, Lessing, Herder and numerous other intellectuals. Today, reincarnation is a very basic doctrine of not only occultists in America but of much of the counter culture as well. Some sociological surveys suggest that almost a quarter of the U.S. population believes in Reincarnation.

Anthropologists tell us that the conception of the transmigration of the soul is an element found world-wide in primitive religions, and is extremely ancient, going back behind the Egyptian religion associated with embalming. The idea of the soul's traveling from body to body is similar to the primitive idea that the soul can leave the body during sleep and experience the activities of dreams. Transmigration, however, refers to the possibility of moving from a human to an animal or insect body, while Reincarnation means moving only from a human to another human body.

Modern Theosophy made Reincarnation a major belief, drawing it from Hinduism, rather than from Plato and the West. The counter-cultural "underground" today regularly speaks of "Karma," "the next life" and in general exhibits a strong theosophical outlook, probably as a reaction against the established churches and their theology. This reaction probably stems from the strong moralism of Christianity rather than from doctrine itself.

The problem I see in a belief in Reincarnation -- including the Karmic doctrine -- is the downgrading such an outlook gives to the world, and the present life, here and now. It is a doctrine of reaction, of apology for the status quo, and a kind of cosmic excuse for turning inward and away from the need of our fellowmen. To a large degree, it is a non-moral, escapist doctrine, very well suited to the particularism, individualism, and lack of involvement taught by both religion and occultism today.

## Pantheism:

Philosophically, Reincarnation also rests on the great pantheistic idea that all thing are bound up together in one whole. The soul is part of nature and, like nature, promises to always survive, although perhaps in a very changed form. To a large degree, Reincarnation serves to pacify the anxieties that plague so many people today, hence its popularity.[16]

## Conclusion

It may be surprising to think that occult self-therapy has a theology, yet since it functions so often as a pseudo-religion, we should expect at least a pseudo-theology. The concepts of dualism, sympathy, elitism, of the second birth, of imitation and self-assertion as well as of reincarnation are found in all forms of occultism. It is safe

to say that there could be no superstition or magic without the
ence of most of these concepts in the minds of those whose theo
doctrines work themselves out in occult practices.

# CHAPTER IV

## OCCULT PRACTICES

The late J. Schoneberg Setzer, former professor of Religion at Ha wick College in up-state New York has contributed greatly to discussion of the relationship of the occult to religion. In an arti in RELIGION IN LIFE on "The God of Ambrose Worrell and of Ed. Cayce",[1] Setzer declared that the Biblical faith was based on E.S. visions, auditions and visits from non-carnate entities.[2] Accord to Professor Setzer, the Bible developed in a context of paranorr experiences, for such mystical events, such as healings, seeing spiri astral projection and viewing the human aura, are the primary pl nomena of religious experience.[3]

Biblical scholars may well disagree with Porfessor Setzer, yet cannot be denied that the Mosaic faith of the Old Testament a the faith in Jesus of the New Testament grew up in the conte of unusual experiences. Even the liberal tradition in theology acknov edges the experiences of men in the Biblical tradition with "t Holy".[4] The experiences of men and women with the holy, "the othe or the Divine has been called a fascination with the tremendous m) tery that puts us in dread and yet lures us on. Moses' experien with the burning bush (Exodus 3:1-4:17), and Peter's encounter wi the power of Jesus in a fishing boat (Luke 5:1-11) illustrate ma: terror of and fascination with the Holy -- as does the experien of Peter and John at the Mount of Transfiguration (Mark 9:2-13).

Modern churches all too often offer little in the way of possibili for men and women to experience the Holy. Fundamentalism, giv( over to nineteenth century Revivalism, turns to self-induced, musi hypnotized emotional experiences as substitutes for that act being grasped by the Holy, which no man can arrange. Roman Cathol cism, moving out of the medieval superstitions that held on for centu ies in Italy, Spain and Portugal, no longer produces many shrin( where miraculous healings take place. Now that the thrust of tl

Protestant Reformation has passed into the willing and abl
of Vatican II Catholic Christians, this mighty company of b
offers less and less of those super-normal experiences th
and women of our time (as in every time) seem to long for.
situation, of the reforming of Catholicism and the rationa
Protestantism, it is not surprising that movements of faith-
glossalalia (speaking in tongues), new religious cults, and of
practices have sprung up.

This is not the place to discuss faith healing and the glossalalia
ment within Christianity. These subjects are well treated else
Although the practices of many Christian groups bear close
blance to occultic practices (spontaneous healings, being
away with the ejaculations of glossalalia or prayer languag
lengthening," and other oddities), we must limit ourselve
to the more exotic practices outside the churches.

**Exorcism:**

The basic dualism of occultism leads its adherents to the
of Animism, the seeing of spirits in rocks, trees, places, a
and people. These spirits can be good, evil, or neutral in pr
religion, but in the modern occultic outlook, it is mainly tl
spirits or demons that are important. This concentration
evil side of the spiritual world, with demonology, is a one
approach to ancient religious ideas that occultists share with
mentalist Christians. One hears a great deal from both groups
"spirit possession" but it is always possession by evil spirit
good spirits. The one-sided emphais of occultists, fundamer
and "Jesus people" on "casting out demons", with a corresp
silence about good spirits or neutral ones (like the neutral
which Socrates said spoke to him, in THE APOLOGY[6]), demon
the partiality -- and morbidity -- of religious outlook in these r
groups.

Within these parameters, we can examine the phenomenon of
cism; the casting out of spirits. Modern occultists, like their
people" counterparts, usually identify demon possession with
negative character factor or social dysfunction. Falling und
grip of alcohol, drugs or other obsessions (for example, to b
a video game freak or compulsive thief) is identified with
possession.

In Christian circles, spirits are cast out by prayer, the laying on of hands and by the use of fragments of the Catholic or Episcopal rites of exorcism. In occultic groups, there are a variety of techniques, depending upon the interest of the participants. Spells, charms, various rituals, the laying on of hands, sprinkling with salt, even the drawing of the pentagram and the invocation of the aid of other spirits, may be involved.

I have witnessed two exorcisms, both at youth meetings where there was a strongly spiritualistic element among the participants. The first involved a young woman who felt a curse had been laid upon her. This "curse" manifested itself in her life, she reported to the group, by her "bad luck" with boy friends. This "bad luck" was somewhat more serious than the usual boy-girl fallings-out, for it took the form of serious auto accidents that befell every boy she dated. This situation, of some long standing, disturbed the girl very much, and she pleaded with the group, in tears, for help in "lifting the curse". The idea of being possessed by a curse is more expressive of the lore of witchcraft than of any other portion of the occult spectrum, but I take it as the equivalent of being possessed by a spirit or demon.

After prayers and affirmations by the group that the curse was even now being broken, the girl was sprinkled with salt and curse pronounced "over", "ended", "cast off". this announcement was sincerely believed by the affected one, and the "exorcism" was greeted by loud shouts and tears of joy by all those present.

Another exorcism was so quietly done that it might have escaped the notice of the people in the same room. I was the leader of a seminar at a youth retreat, and noted what happened, I suppose, only because I knew what to look for. A young person was complaining of a sore throat that was spoiling his fun during the retreat. Another young person, after some time, told the sufferer that he could heal the problem by casting out the evil spirit that was afflicting him. The first youth did not pick up on this offer at first, nor did he reject the idea. The "healer" repeated the offer after a while and the "sufferer" accepted it. I was sitting some distance away amid a good deal of noise, but was able to see the "healer" touch the "sufferer", and repeat several sentences. Later, I spoke to the boy with the sore throat, inquiring about his health. He reported that the soreness was gone.

The elements that make up an exorcism seem two-fold. First, the belief that some state of affairs (illness, bad luck) is the result of the intervention of spiritual forces in one's life. Secondly, the belief that faith in a power greater than this invading spiritual power can overcome the "demon". No matter what the ritual involved may be like, these two beliefs underlie all exorcism.

## Tarot Cards:

The investigation of one's inward self, of the strengths and weaknesses of one's character, as well as the search for clues to the decisions and actions to be taken in the future is done by many by the use of the Tarot cards. The Tarot deck is the ancestor of the common playing cards of today, probably introduced into Europe from Persia by wandering bands of "Gypsies" around 1300 A.D. The Gypsies, according to a generally accepted theory, came to Europe from India by way of Persia. In Europe, decks of cards developed in a form called "tarots," containing 78 cards. Fifty-six of these were in suits similar to card decks of today, and twenty-two were symbolic picture cards used in fortune telling. The suit cards were named "the lesser arcana" and the picture cards, "the greater arcana". Every picture card had a symbolic significance that bore a meaning along, and in concert with, the other cards, for the adept at fortune telling. Eventually, card games were invented, the deck reduced to fifty-two cards, plus one of the cards in the greater arcana, the joker.

I have witnessed attempts to tell fortunes with ordinary playing cards in the military service and in college, and found these singularly unimpressive, although occult literature gives instructions for the use of such decks. More impressive is the use of the Tarot or greater arcana which is becoming generally available now that popular interest in the occult is high.

Playing cards have been a part of the everyday life of the common people for many centuries. They provide entertainment for elderly people, pastimes for the sick and form part of the equipment of the soldier. Cards are not always used just for entertainment or gambling. Even in the relative low culture of the Southern mountains, we find the hill-billy song that speaks of the soldier in the guardhouse who uses his deck of cards as a Bible. In this sentimental song, the various cards are given symbolic values relating to Scripture. It is not unusual, then, that cards are resorted to by many as aids in predicting the future. Wherever people interested in the occult are gathered, we will see either Tarot or regular playing cards.

So widespread is the use of the Tarot deck today that a person inclined towards the occult who felt he had a problem might very well resort to the cards for help first. Such a use of cards is technically called divination. Divination has a long and honorable history in all religions throughout all time. In the Bible the Hebrews sought to divine God's will through the use of lots, while King Saul, cut off from the fellowship of the prophet Samuel, sought out the Witch of Endor who raised the ghost of Samuel by a forbidden practice of divination called necromancy. The Greeks and Romans thought they could divine the future by reading signs in the entrails of animals. Among the Stone Age people of New Guinea and the Bush tribes of Africa, the future is told by the casting of bones, sticks and rocks, which are read by the configuration of the pattern in which they fall.

Divination among modern occultists might begin with the cards and go on to be used in conjuction with the casting of horoscopes, a study of the numerological significance of various names and dates, capped off with meditations. There is one thing about religion of any kind, including occult religion; the faithful does not give up easily. If the desired assistance does not come through one technique then another is used. If this does not seem very religious; it may be because of the basic manipulative nature of occultism as well as because many occultists do not believe their practices entail anything supernatural, but rather are reflective of the inner life of a person. If one does not find his clue by one route then another practice may lead him to a richer depth by touching another psychological level.

There are various means by which Tarot and regular cards are used to analyze character, or predict the future. There is a method of using the full pack of the Tarot, of using only a partial pack and of using ordinary cards, either the full deck or just the face cards. There are a number of different patterns in which the cards are laid, including the pattern of the cross.

One method of using Tarot cards is to put a mental question forward, then lay out the cards like this:

One might take the cards, shuffle them from right to left, cut them, then choose ten cards at random which are then randomly put back into the pack, which is shuffled and cut three more times.

Ten cards are dealt face down and they are read by turning them over one at a time, each one corresponding to the following clues about probable events in the future.

The first two cards symbolize the person's state of mind. The next card symbolizes the person's influence over others. Included in this portion of the reading might be the answer to the subject's question as to how his problem would be resolved. The next two cards symbolize obstacles to the subject's goals. The rest of the cards symbolize the future outcome of the person's problem and give clues to the probable attainment or missing of the subject's life goals.

## Palmistry:

One of the more enduring symbols of the occult aspect of life in every society is the fortune-teller's or palm-reader's sign. We have all seen it, in small towns, large cities and along the highways in front of trailers out in the open country. These "spiritual leaders" as they often call themselves, usually read the palm of their clients although cards and the crystal ball are sometimes used. Depending upon their location in the country, these spiritual leaders may take on the trappings of the Christian religion, the Gypsy, or the Indian medicine man. In Negro areas, the witch-woman or spiritual leader may take on some unique characteristics, but in general, readers servicing black people are oriented toward Christianity. What does a person expect to learn from examining lines in the palm of a hand? essentially we may say that occultic practice bases itself on the belief that all things are joined together and influence each other. The belief in the wholeness and inter-connectiveness of all things is actually a very healthy thing when it is understood with reference to the doctrine of God as Creator and providential sustainer of all that exists. However, in occult practice this vision of the unity of things is taken as a warrant for belief that all things are determined in advance and consequently that one is helpless in the face of the predestination of his life.

Palmistry is laid out along the same lines as astrology since various parts of the hand are said to be ruled by certain of the planets. According to those who practice this occult science there are two parts to the study of the human hand, chirosophy and chirognomy. Chirosophy refers to the significance of the lines of the hand and the interpretations of the pads or mounts at the base of the fingers and thumb. Chirognomy refers to the interpretation of the shape of the hand and its fingers. Probably most people interested in the occult incline towards the interpretation of the lines of hand. Most people are familiar with the terms, "life-line", "heart-line", and "head-line", which are the creases of the palm. These lines are assimulated to the belief that these and other lines determine the length of one's life; one's success in romance and accomplishments in life. The number of times one will fall in love and major illnesses are all said to be marked in the palm.

## Assorted Divinatory Practices:

Since occultism has been practiced all over the world for thousands of years, it is not remarkable that there should be literally hundreds of different ways that people seek to analyze character and predict the future. I mention some of these here in brief rather than giving a full analysis of each practice.

**Tea-leaf reading,** a commonly met with practice, rests upon the interpretation of patterns made by the residual tea leaves in the bottom of a client's cup.

An unusual practice is **Moleosophy,** or the study of moles. The idea here is that the location of the moles on the body will give clues to the character and future prospects of the person. An example of the interpretation of a mole might be that if one has a mole on the lip, that person has a benevolent nature. This particular practice is not very widespread, and reveals some of the more far-fetched ideas that turn up in the occult. Traditionally, witches are said to have warts, moles, and cold or "dead" spots on their bodies.

**Ouija boards** originated as a parlor game; a function they still fulfill for people of all ages. "Ouija" comes from a melting together of the French and German words for **yes.** The idea behind the Ouija is that the plachete or moving wooden finger rest is guided either by the subconscious mind or by spirits. As it moves over the game board, which includes the alphabet and numbers, as well as yes and no; it is believed that messages are spelled out and that the answers to questions are given. Probably most people who use the ouija board do so in fun, but there are those who take it seriously, and I've heard many reports of people who were frightened by the "messages" they received.

**The interpretation of people's names,** either by the translation of the letters of the name into **numeralogical equivalents** or by referring to the original meaning of the name, is another minor occult practice. Of course the idea that names have reality is very old and forms part of the background of the Christian religion. All religions view names as having a power in and of themselves which can be called upon by the faithful. The name of God is holy and thus had an efficacious power, a belief which is echoed to this day in the Invocation of God at the beginning of a worship service and in the closing of Christian prayers with the name of Jesus Christ, as well as in the Benediction that generally closes all worship services. There is a general belief, in primitive forms of religion, in the power of the personal name. For example, in some primitive cultures, one never allows his true name to become generally known for fear that someone might use his name to work a harmful spell against him. As we know from the custom of the American Indians, a person earns his own name after passing through rites of initiation that admit him to the company of adults of the tribe.

Even among enlightened Christian people there is a strong tendency to take names very seriously, as there are books in circulation that give the original meaning of names in Hebrew, Greek, German, etc., which are often consulted when Christian children are named. We have a general feeling that names do mean something, which is reflected in the kinds of names that are given to villians and comic characters in movies and plays.

Perhaps the commonest manipulation of names in an occultic way is to translate the letters of the name into some sort of numerical equivalent, which can be as simple as "a equals 1, b equals 2," or can rest on some more complicated scheme.

Once a name is translated into numbers, we move into the area of **numerology**. Numerology is the occult science of the meaning of numbers. Numbers have fascinated man from the time of their development, as seen in Pythagoras, an ancient Greek philosopher, who felt that all things were created of numbers. We know the prevalence of numbers as important symbols throughout human history. In the Book of Revelation we find that the beast of the pit is said to have a numerical identification, "666". This book of visions contains many references to numbers, including seven angels, three woes, seven plagues, seven bowls of wrath and twenty-four elders. However, the reference in Revelation 13:18 to "666" is the clearest influence of numerological occultism on Scripture. Modern scholars have demonstrated that "666" is a cryptic reference to "Nero, Caesar."

In our day numbers play symbolic roles over wide areas of our culture. We speak of "7-up"; remark that things are "No. 1"; think of the number seven as lucky; and of the number 13 as unlucky. In general there is so much belief that the use of numbers is scientific today that we often miss the symbolic or magical influence of such expressions as "the 400"; "the upper 10 percent", and "the upper half" of the class. There are elaborate schemes in numerology for taking a person's birthdate, his name reduced to a numerical equivalent and the equivalent number of the day on which the reading is made, and reducing the whole formula to a mystical number that is supposed to give a message for the person for that day. I know that these practices are followed by some today, but it is my impression that other forms of occultic readings are more widespread.

## Reading the Human Aura:

The occultist, and the counter cultural person in general, shares the desire expressed by Carlos Castaneda in his books on Don Juan: the desire "to see". "To see" means more than to look and see what is before us as phenomena in the world, it means to see behind, within, to probe to the mystical depths of the reality we are and which surrounds us. Occultism, in its various forms, teaches man "to see", and, indeed, this "seeing" is part of the healing process in occult self-therapy.

There are many things we may learn (or "unlearn") to see: ghosts, spirits, vibrations, powers, but the commonest phenomena occultists may "see" are human auras. Perhaps the reader is not familiar with the term or the concept. If so, here is a short introduction to the aura.

The aura is (supposedly) an emanation of light arising from the surface of the human body, as well as from animal and vegetable bodies, while these bodies are living. Oscar Bagnall has written an interesting little book on THE ORIGIN AND PROPERTIES OF THE HUMAN AURA.[7] Bagnall is scientifically trained and his work is as much a study of optics, vision and the properties of light, as it is an examination of the aura. He places the claims of ancient religion (about haloes, and faces shining, as in Moses' case) and of occultists on a scientific basis. Essentially, Bagnall proves, as recent Soviet researchers in photography have proved, that an aura, or haze of light is emitted by living things and that disturbances to the living body show up in this aura or haze. Bagnall, like the physician, Walter J. Kilner, before him, developed dye-treated screens with which to examine this aura.

Bagnall discovered that the use of certain dye-screens sensitized his eyes so that he could see, in a dim light, waves of ultrashort wavelength (ultra violet rays). He soon discovered that his own hands and the heads and bodies of his friends were surrounded by a haze (the aura) composed of just such light rays. It became clear that these rays were visible only to the nightseeing nerves of the retina, the rods. In the main, one can bring these retinal rods into play, in a dim light, by peering out of the corners (sides) of the eyes -- as everyone taught the principles of seeing during night-fighting in the Armed Forces knows.

Bagnall makes belief in the existence of the aura respectable. He does not, of course, validate much of the religious and occultic lore that surrounds the "seeing" of a person's aura. It is possible to barely make out this "haze" of light around a living body, in dim light, by looking out of the corner of the eye, if you have a natural talent for it -- by which I suppose I mean having very sensitive retinal rods. It seems possible that some men and women through the ages have had this talent for sensitivity and have built up the legends of the halo, the aura and the shining presence, or nimbus, upon it.

Not all modern occultists claim to be able to see the human aura, although most believe in it and put some store in the possibility of making "readings" of one's state of health and mind from it. Other occultists do claim the ability to discern it and use it in their interpretation of character, susceptibility to illness, and the presence of mental or moral problems.

The aura appears to have an inner, brighter area, which is about the same thickness in everyone, and an outer, fainter area, which is less distinct and fades off, extending out beyond the body. This outer haze is much thicker in women than in men and also is said to assume various configurations according to the health and mental condition of the person. Both Bagnall and Dr. Kilner, as well as modern occultists, claim to be able to diagnose diseases, mental disturbances and pregnancy from changes in the human aura.

The aura is generally gray, although it may appear to be lighter or darker in various individuals. Some occultists claim that auras are colored red, blue, and even black, but Bagnall's experiments do not support this. According to one current occultic version, persons with dark auras are inclined to evil, and people with light-colored auras are committed to good.

## Tuning In To The Infinite Wholeness:

In order to fully understand the inner reason of the occultic world view and thus see the logic involved in the practices already discussed and those we are about to analyze, we must bear in mind the basic occult philosophy that sees the universe as a living whole of which each person is a part and in whom all the grand structures of the universe are duplicated on a smaller scale. The person is a microcosm of the macrocosm, and between him and everything else that exists, visible and invisible, there are living links or vibrations. These links are illustrated in the beliefs that one's life history is written in the lines of the hand, marked in the moles on his body, to be deduced from his name or from numbers derived from his name or birthdate, and even to be seen reflected in the patterns which cards or tea-leaves take in his presence.

Underlying this basic belief that "all is one" is a further belief that the everyday waking form of consciousness is somehow a distortion of reality, a confusion in which we are cut off from the great stream of things that is the really real. The occultist would say that the so-called scientific worldview is inadequate for it does not account for all sorts of everyday phenomena such as wordless communication between people, known technically as ESP, or spiritual healings, except on a psychological basis.

In the now famous trilogy about the teachings of Don Juan, by Carlos Castenada,[8] the emphasis upon the artificial quality of the ordinary experience of the world is stressed. Don Juan finally gets Castenada to see that his so-called rational and logical outlook on life is but an interpretation of the events of the world that Castenada has been initiated into from birth. Our belief in cause and effect, in a materialistic explanation for events; our expectation that there is a reason for everything that happens that fits into our worldview; all this is not actually the truth or an example of reality according to Don Juan, but is conditioned or learned behavior on our part. It takes a long time for Castenada to understand and accept this premise. Eventually, he does accept it, and finds that such an understanding does enable him to move into "a separate reality" where "he can stop the world" and the most unlikely events become experiences he can and must accept. We need to note that Castenada is not the first person to give support to the occultic worldview, for the philosopher David Hume, known as the father of the empiricistic outlook, long ago pointed out that there is no reality to cause and effect, but that it is simply a matter of the habit of our minds and the selectivity of our thinking.

The entire intellectual experience in America since World War II has contained a heavy element of dissatisfaction with the adequacy of the scientific outlook to explain, shape and aid in the solution to the problems man encounters in every area of his life. The lack of attention to the specifically human interests and needs of men and women in formal psychology has given rise to Humanistic Psychology. The inability of even modern theories of physics to account for all the data in the study of the atom, and even of the stars, has brought dissatisfaction to the minds of many physicists. The enigma of the riddle of Shroeder's cat in quantum physics seems to leave the universe open to interpretation as a place with multitudes of separate realities. The experience of not being able to cover the deeply experienced problems of human will and action by the categories of academic philosophy has brought about the spread of existentialistic ideas among philosophers and intellectuals in all fields. The almost insoluble moral issues connected with race, war, poverty and ecology has led to a strong bent towards mysticism among people in both the scientific and humanistic camps. Years ago C. P. Snow could write that there were "two cultures" the scientific and the humanistic, with no communication between them.[9] After the experiences of the peace struggle and the onset of anxiety over the environment, such a division is no longer a general fact of life. At a myriad number of points, the traditional, rational worldview seems to have broken down, and this makes the occultic alternative more acceptable than it has been to intellectuals in several centuries. Verbal exponents of the occult are able to point out the shortcomings of a rational outlook with relative ease. This makes the teachings of mystics, astrologers and even witches seem much more plausible than ever before.

In religion, too, the turning of the confessional bases of Christianity into systems of rational propositions that could be taught to the clergy in systematic theologies and to the laity in catechisms, was probably in tune with the general outlook of the eighteenth and nineteenth century, particularly after the destruction of the first World War. It became clear to millions that the teachings of Christianity, framed in such systems, sounded good but failed to work. Karl Barth, Paul Tillich and others tried to bring about a revolution in theology, each along different lines, in order to recapture the living essence of faith. All too often the new attempts to existential-

ze Christianity became new orthodoxies and thus brought about
he dissatisfaction that a failure to be helpful always brings to the
minds of thoughful people. The present emphasis upon spirituality,
aith healing, speaking in tongues and other experiential phenomena
s part of the reaction today to the lack of attention to human needs
n formal theology.

Over the past several decades the living practice of religion was
skewed by the explosion of the civil rights issue. For many the practice of religion came to be involvement in the social struggle; for
millions of others, it became a close attention to everything else
in the church but the social issue. In all this the deep-seated emotional needs of persons got lost. The heavy emphasis upon personal
experience in religion today is directly related to this recent failure
to take personal, individual needs seriously.

## Consciousness Raising

The essential clue to the often found practical utility of occultic
practices lies in their ability to modify or raise consciousness. In
this respect occultism shares the experiential grounding and gives
the personal "benefits" of both religion and drug use. To the existen-
tial participant, everything in his world can be changed by the shift
in consciousness or "high" that such activity can bring. Mankind
seems to be an animal with an implacable urge to experience modifica-
tions of consciousness. Everything from sex to toys and games are
employed in this quest, which you can prove for yourself by looking
through a kalaidescope or playing a fast game of touch football.
As necessary as the material dimension is, man basically cares more
for his experience of consciousness than he does for food and shelter.
People will go hungry and wander the roads without homes (as Jesus
and Buddha did) looking for a new experience of consciousness, whereas a new experience of consciousness will not necessarily drive men
to a new material relation to the world.

I have been working with the idea of "consciousness" and " states
of consciousness" for many years. Long before the rise of publicity
about "Consciousness III", I identified and analyzed "The New Mentality". I have come to recognize the reality of this new state of consciousness and to ascertain that there are stages, higher and higher
within it.

One of the ways in which a state of consciousness is changed is to
become aware that one does exist in a state of consciousness that

can be changed. Many people are unaware that this is a fact and seem to consider the way their minds work as ultimate reality, unavailable for change. Once one becomes aware that the way in which we see the world is subject to change then perhaps for the first time the person can take thought and begin to shift his appreciation and perspective.

From the beginning of time the link between man's everyday waking state and his unconscious mind has been through his dreams. In dreams that which was forgotten calls itself to our attention, and if consistently ignored forces itself ever back again through repetition. Ultimately, the dreams we ignore may influence us more than the dreams we pay attention to. Without doubt one's consciousness can be raised rather quickly by paying attention to one's dreams.

All forms of psychotherapeutic help take dreams seriously. In Jungian analysis one is usually instructed to keep a record of his dreams. Freud was able to find clues to the inner life of his patients by an interpretation of the symbols that appeared in their dreams. It should be expected then that dreams and their interpretation would play a role in the life of the occultist.

There are two ways of examining one's dreams, the first, in an effort to find clues to one's character and psychological history; the second, in a more occultic vein as a search for clues to the future. It is interesting to note that in the same period of time that has seen a development of the scientific techniques of dealing with the future, the ancient belief in divination has grown up in parallel among all sorts of groups. Douglas McFerran, writing in COMMONWEAL, observes that one of the most curious features of communes, even strictly Christian ones, is the dependence of such people on the techniques of divination as the basis for group decisions.[10]

One might very well ask why there is such stress upon the attempt to read the future today? I see it as having twin prongs, one, as a desire to escape from the single level of existence which is the stress of conscious planning in the scientific worldview, which has led us to a one-level materialistic culture; and the second as an attempt to find a new, more satisfying relationship of the conscious to the unconscious mind. People are not satisfied with things as they are and are seeking freedom outside the bounds of scientific method and the dogmatic contents of traditional religion. Pressed between the rapid technological changes that call all relationships into question and the innovating materialism that characterizes our society as a whole, men and women seek to find some freedom and joy in a state of suspension of disbelief and the rapturous state of consciousness such a suspension can bring.

There are several major schools of dream interpretation that have heavily influenced occultic practice in our time. **Oneiromancy,** or divination by means of the dream, is as old as mankind, and has been known throughout recorded history as well as discovered among the primitive people still existing in the world today. It is well known that the ancient Greeks and Romans believed that the gods spoke to them in dreams and that in the Bible itself, many revelations came to characters in both the Old and new Testaments through dreams. We can immediately think of the dreams that came to Abraham in Genesis 15 (note verse 12), the dream of Joseph in Genesis 37:5ff, Joseph's interpretation of dreams in Genesis 40 and 41, as well as Jacob's dream (Gen. 32). In the New Testament, we immediately think of Pilate's wife's dream (Matthew 27:19), Peter's vision in Acts 10, and Paul's dream of a man of Macedonia in Acts 16:9 Joseph is told by God in a dream to marry Mary, and later told to flee into Egypt with the infant, Jesus, again in a dream (Matt. 1-2ff).

Mircea Eliade declares that it is not possible to explain a myth or to reduce dreams to a single explanation. He declares that the myth, because it has universal applicability, gets closer to the general feelings and apprehensions of mankind, but says that there is a continuity between the world of dreams and the world of the myth. The categories of space and time are modified in dreams similarly to their transcendence in myths. It is not surprising that there is a spiritual or religious dimension to dreams since it is the nature of religious experience to stir up and to grow out of the depths of a person's personality. No matter how civilized we may think ourselves to be there is something disturbing and significant about any dream that we may remember. While dreams are individual and not social, and therefore cannot be religious in the broad sense, each of us, nevertheless, has a kind of basic feeling that the depths of our being and the source of the holy lie close together. Eliade, in MYTHS, DREAMS AND MYSTERIES[11] follows an interpretation of dreams that sees in the content and structure of the unconsciousness a result of racial memories, representing constantly recurring critical events throughout the existence of mankind. This is derived from the pioneering work of Jung and is very similar to much of the interpretation that takes place in occultism.

Perhaps the most usual form of interpretation of dreams in Western society today is the specifically sexual interpretation of Sigmund Freud. Few of us have escaped the pan-sexuality of Freud's interpretations because of the widespread publicity given Freud's work. There is little reason to doubt that a great deal of the imagery of dreams and a large part of man's psychic life is tied up with sexual elements; considering the physiological basis of personality it could hardly be otherwise, but the one-sided interpretation of every symbol in dreams as having a specifically sexual connotation has been legitimately rejected in our time. In Freudian dream interpretation, every pointed object becomes an indicator of male sex and every round or hollow object a symbol of female sexuality. These insights may often be true, but just as often they impress us as being a straight jacket with which everything is bound so that no other dimensions of truth may appear. perhaps a more damning critique is one that sees sexual interpretation alone as an utter failure to break through a materialistic interpretation of even the most mystical experiences we have.

The modern world of the occult would probably not be possible without the legitimazation and explanatory quality given mystical experience by the work of C. G. Jung. Jung brought the sensitivity of an artist and the insights of a psychoanalyst to the whole area of occultic phenomena. He was sufficiently convinced of the importance of occultic phenomena to resist the distaste of Freud for such interests.

Jung saw that the various systems of mysticism and the beliefs and activities of occult groups touched on some real needs and insights of human beings. He saw that man could not live by a physiological interpretation of his feelings alone but must have the mythic substructure of his life recognized and taken into account in the direction of his life. In order to do this, Jung developed the idea of the racial memory, found in all human beings, which was populated by so-called archetypical images that crystallized the results of critical experiences that happened over and over again to human beings in every time and every place. These archetypical images included the picture of the wise old man, the mandala or symbol of universal unity, the hero, the trickster and those of beauty and the beast. These figures, which Jung said turn up in everyone's dreams, are also found in the myths and folklore of people everywhere. We are all vaguely familiar with such figures for they form part of the culture of whatever people we happen to come from. Of course in doing this, Jung has identified the world of the myth and world of the dream and has made the dream an entry into the world of religion.

Such support from a widely respected intellectual could not go un-noticed by the occult world. Indeed, Jung's support was at once the expression of the rising need to take this inner life seriously as well as a boost in respectability for such interest. It is not a simple, one-way proposition, but rather a case of universal feeling coming to expression both un Jung and in the ready acceptance of Jung as teacher. It is an illustration of Jung's concept of synchronicity.

Occultism found that a very large amount of its interpretation of dream experiences was underwritten by Jung's studies. At the same time it also absorbed some of the sexual interpretation put forward by Freud and his disciples. As a general knowledge of psychology and psychoanalytic interpretation spread, the recommendation and advice of occult teachers began to sound more and more like the discourse of the psychiatrists.

In dreams, it is generally agreed, a more basic dimension of the person-ality announces itself. Since this part of the self is not subject to the everyday masking effect of social inhibition and deceit, it is almost universally believed to give reliable, if confusing, knowledge about one's life.

In Freudianism, because of the basic commitment to sexuality as the overriding basis for disturbances of the psyche, usually the conflict between the super-ego, the ego and id is seen in the symbolism of dreams. In Jungian analysis, the interpretor may find an expression of the anima or the female element in the male psyche, or the animus, the male element in a female psyche. In occultism, the symbolism of dreams is often taken as expressing some direct purpose or intention and not just as announcing the presence of a suppressed desire or personality element.

Occultic interpretation may take dreams very literally, seeing, for example, a dream of travel as an expression for a desire for freedom, and dreams of falling, as denoting worry.

In occultism not only are dreams taken quite literally, but they are taken as indications of what the future may be like. Just how the sequences of dream pictures are interpreted will depend upon the psychic reader. We should note that dreams are usually interpreted in connection with several other means of divination such as Tarot cards, palm reading and the casting of horoscopes.

## The I-Ching: Throwing the Sticks

There are any number of practices by which men and women seek to divine the future. It is possible to attempt this by the use of dice, a ring attached to a string and used as a pendulum, by the methods involving cards, that we have discussed above, as well as by reading the palm of the hand and similar interpretations of parts of the body. Some of the forms of divination used in the past resurrected in this period of occult interest stagger the imagination. There is **aeromancy** or divination by means of clouds' shapes and other heavenly phenomena. There are **fortune cookies** with messages written on slips baked in them, which are later read at random. There is the study of smoke rising from a fire called **capnomancy**. Indeed, there are few things, animal, plant or mineral, that have not been used or may not be used now to seek clues to future events. Perhaps one of the oldest and most interesting is the **I-Ching**, consisting of the casting of sticks or coins which are interpreted according to the pattern they fall into by reference to the ancient Book of Changes. The Book of Changes, called in Chinese, "I", was probably bought into existence around 1150 B.C. The interpretation of the various patterns into which the traditional sticks of the I-Ching can fall already existed in part before 1150 B.C., but King Wen drew older materials together and produced the present classic about that time.[12] The true name of the book of divinations is "I", which may be interpreted as easy, changing, or constant. The idea of "easy" lies in the more direct oracle involved in casting sticks as opposed to interpreting the patterns of sacred tortoise shells, which was the more ancient form of divination in China.

In modern America the I-Ching has been popularized by the hippie subculture or counter culture because of the oriental influence on the West Coast and the rejection of modern science that underlies so much of the new consciousness. Now the I-Ching is so fully blended into the new sub-culture that the "divining symbols" are printed on cards that can be consulted for the meaning of all 64 ancient hexagrams.

To consult the I-Ching, one takes a handful of sticks and casts them, the result being a randomly formed pattern. This is compared with the hexagram described in the Book of Changes, which furnishes an interpretation. There is an alternative way of doing this, more popular with the young than the sticks; the flipping of coins, particularly Chinese coins. The various arrangements of heads and tails are read as analogous to the patterns formed by the sticks and are similarly interpreted.

When the hexagrams are formed by the sticks or coins and they are looked up in the book, the interpretations are as cryptic to a modern mind as the patterns themselves. One hexagram may be interpreted "Pigs and Fishes" and another "He Treads on the Tiger's Tail". These messages must be further interpreted, and a very large literature has sprung up, giving further interpretation. Indeed, the whole I-Ching ritual might be seen as a method of meditation. In all events, for those who have studied it, it is a way of directing life and divining the future.

## Astrology

I have deliberately waited until the last to discuss astrology, for astrology is a foundation stone of almost all the other occult "sciences". The practice of astrology goes back to the earliest days of man of which we have any kinds of record. The zodiac, or the stylized representation of the horizon marked by twelve signs, comes to us from the ancient Middle East, having had its rise among the Babylonians and Assyrians and having been influenced by the ancient Egyptians. Astrology is also anciently known in China and India and thus forms a kind of inner core for an ancient universal religion that was also echoed among the Aztecs and Incas as well as other tribes around the world.

Astrology is based upon the belief that everything influences everything else. Its foundation is a concept of sympathy and cosmic integration. In modern times those interested in astrology have attempted to give something of a scientific rationale by speaking of the sun as the center of the solar system and also as the center of the life forces that animate everyone.

The form of astrology in general practice today is **natal** or **birth astrology**. This is the basis for the horoscopes that fill our newstands, keyed as they are to a span of several weeks, covering the birthdates of the year with the twelve signs of the zodiac. Of course the commercial horoscopes are shot-gun affairs, which even astrology buffs declare are very crude because they are designed to cover an assumed average of people born between two dates, some three or four weeks apart. Individual horoscopes are supposedly carefully cast to represent the positions of the stars, planets, sun and moon at the exact minute

one was born. According to the modern explanation of the "imprinting" character of the planetary positions, the air we breathe first
in our lives is charged with particles magnetized by the sun and
the various heavenly bodies and this gives us the peculiar personality
construct that is attributed to the various sun-signs such as Aries
or Taurus.

## The Sun-Signs

The term astrology means the science of the stars. In ancient times,
running right up to the Renaissance, astrology included the scientific
study now known as astronomy. Indeed, the possibility of making
rather exact observations of the movements of the planets, which
wobble and shift along the horizon and thus have received their
name, **planetos,** or wanderers, led men in the past as well as now
to seriously consider astrology an exact science. It is well known
that the position of the planets and the stars can be predicted for
years, so it was not difficult to suppose that this exactitude of meas-
urement might also be true for one's personal life history as well.
We must remember that in ancient times the distinction between
sound theory about natural phenomena and a superstition or fantastic
connection was unknown. Among all so-called prescientific peoples,
the very basis of scientific reasoning is harmony or sympathy, the
idea that life influences life.

According to the ancients the night sky was marked by twelve stellar
constellations. These constellations, beginning with Aries, which
is supposedly dominant from March 21 - April 19, and running to
Pisces, which dominates from February 20 - March 20, contain the
powers that marks the characteristics of the personalities born during
their period of sway.

The twelve signs of the Zodiac are thus distributed throughout the
population according to the birthdates of people. One would expect
that the traditional wisdom about the kind of person that an Aries
or Taurus was supposed to be, would prove to be very inexact and
unreliable. However, as strange as it seems, people often do exhibit
the kind of characteristics their sun-signs call for whether they
are interested in astrology or not. It is perhaps this odd fact of
the amazing coincidences between the declared characteristics
of the sun-sign and the actual facts of human nature that make
astrology a disturbing possibility for many modern people. We are
at a loss to explain why the Aries person should be headstrong and

aggressive, but in many instances all we can do is accept this as a fact.

The twelve sun-signs and their characteristics are:

Aries, or the Ram, March 21 - April 19 -- the Aries personality is intelligent, creative, adaptive, courageous and pioneering. It is also impetuous and headstrong and disdains routine work.

Taurus, or the Bull, April 20 - May 19 -- the Taurus personality is strong, even stubborn and unchangeable. Taurus persons are ruled by their emotions and they seek creature comforts. Where Aries is idealistic in thought, Taurus is practical.

Gemini, or the Twins, May 20 - June 20 -- as might be supposed, Gemini is a sign of adaptibility and versatility. There is a kind of duality in them so that they fit in anywhere. The tend to be clever and witty and very popular.

Cancer, or the Crab, sometimes called the Moon Child today, June 21 - July 22 -- Cancer people are home-loving and domestic while also enjoying travel. They tend to be imaginative, affectionate and basically conservative.

Leo the Lion, July 23 - August 21 -- Leo is the sign of strong personality, born leadership. There is ambition and idealism mixed with positive thinking, but also some impulsiveness that can seek domination without thought for others. Leos often exert strong influence on other people.

Virgo the Virgin, August 22 - September 22 -- This is the planet Mercury's sign, which makes for quickness of disposition. Virgos tend to be great talkers with inquiring minds. Their minds run through analysis and comparison, while their emotions make them sympathetic to the problems of others. One major weakness is fault-finding.

Libra, or the Scales, September 23 - October 22 -- This is the sign of balance, ruled by Venus, giving Libras a love of harmony. They are strong fighters for justice and can become steadfast in opposing what they see as wrong. They make good researchers and inventors.

Scorpio the Scorpion, October 23 - November 21 -- This sign is governed by Mars and is an enterprising, fearless sign. Rather quiet in manner, when stirred up, Scorpios become very aggressive. Their weakness is that they become domineering and walk over the rights of others.

Sagittarius, the Archer, November 22 - December 21 -- Governed by Jupiter, Sagittarius is a sign of busyness and natural energy. Hardworkers, they create much good, yet have the weakness of impulsiveness.

Capricorn, the Goat, December 22 - January 21 -- The intellectual sign, with the characteristics of the philosopher. They tend to love being alone and are capable of planning and organization. Their weakness is a trend toward pessimism and moodiness.

Aquarius, the Water-Bearer, January 22 - February 19 -- is the sign of frank and friendly people who are interested in the betterment of mankind. Many poets, pioneers and scientists have been born under this sign, giving rise to the belief that the Age of Aquarius is to be a time when wisdom and love come to control the world.

Pisces, the Fish, February 20 - March 20 -- This is a modest sign of generous people. Pisces are cautious and optimistic at the same time. They are calm and trusting, but their trusting nature often becomes a weakness due to the over-estimation of the knowledge of others and lack of confidence in themselves.

## Some Tales of the Sun-Signs

During 1969 and early 1970, I was doing the research that resulted in the book, RELIGION IN THE AGE OF AQUARIUS.[13] As part of this research I investigated my own horoscope, securing numerous books on the topic and ordering a "Personal Time Pattern" from the Time Pattern Research Institute.[14] This personal horoscope I followed very carefully, guarding myself from self-fulfilling prophecies by reading the message for the day just before going to sleep at night. In this way I hoped to be able to judge how accurately the horoscope was without letting it affect my approach to the problems of the day. During the month of January, there was a particularly severe ice condition on the roads in our area of Kentucky. I naturally took precautions to guard against accidents, including the use of snow tires and chains. Despite adverse weather, my precautions were successful until one evening when returning home from work. I was driving very slowly in my station wagon when it began to slip dangerously on the ice. Nothing I did could bring it under control, and it picked up speed going down a small hill. Suddenly a truck appeared around a curve and I struck it head-on, demolishing the car. The car was totally wrecked, although I was amazingly unhurt. Later that night, getting into bed, I read my horoscope. It said, "You appear to be somewhat accident prone, for which reason you should try to avoid running any undue risk of mishap when traveling. . ."

During the rest of the year many other readings for the day were extremely close to actual events, so that it was difficult to simply explain some of these messages as pure coincidence.

In the case of a close friend of mine, a physician, his introduction to occultism was rather dramatic. During his residency in Denver, he was present in the emergency room with several other doctors when a young woman was brought in with slashed wrists. This girl was under the influence of drugs and behaved in a wild manner, preventing treatment. My friend retreated to a far wall but the patient saw him and suddenly calmed down. Her first clear statement was "You can help me. . . you're an Aquarius." My friend didn't know if he was or not, but did treat her. Later, thinking about the incident, he checked his sun-sign. He was, indeed, an Aquarius.

**Harry.** Let us call him simply "Harry". He is a free person, a full person; even more than that, Harry is a happening. Around 55 years old, gray with a full head of Beatle-length hair, widely expanded around the middle, Harry, at first sight, is an unlikely youth culture hero. Yet Harry is -- and more, he is an unofficial missionary to the counter-culture at large, spreading the Word to hitchhikers picked up one by one all over the country. Christian though he is, Harry belongs in a study of the use of the occult as a means to healing, for Harry's tool is his psychic ability.

I realize that one never knows what to think about secondhand reports of "occult" phenomena, yet I must say that Harry has the most amazing "ESP" or psychic ability I have ever run across, in books or in personal experience. He can look at you and tell you everything you ever did. Such a talent sweeps the average youth right off his feet. People believe in Harry -- and they seem to do it instantaneously.

I think Harry enjoys his psychic powers. Surely he is to be admired for the raport with the young he is able to establish by the use of them. He is kind and generous to a fault, and his prayers and friendships have helped many people. I know some of these people and go on their reports, not Harry's, in making this judgment. Harry uses his mind-reading ability to set up a relationship with people, then begins to preach about Christ, forgiveness, and love. His batting average in the spiritual ball game is high.

Harry's presence seems to bring a sense of peace and to result in feelings of freedom and joy in the people he reaches. I have witnessed a large segment of a University community quite literally transformed by Harry's work. Looking at this group one being to understand what the Gospel means when it declares:

"You shall cast out demons in my name."

Harry is chief engineer for a large manufacturing concern in the Middle West, and travels extensively in pursuit of both his vocation and his avocation. Once, several years ago, he and his wife planned a vacation trip to Florida. On the day before they were to leave some teenagers in their community (who only knew Harry slightly) were working with a Ouija board. Suddenly the Ouija spelled out a message saying that Harry was going on an automobile trip on which his car would strike a telephone pole. The crash would not harm him but would trigger a heart attack. Harry was going to die if he took that trip. The young people didn't know what to do. Then one timidly phoned Harry's wife and gave her the message. Not knowing how to deal with it, she called her pastor. He suggested that Harry should go ahead and make the trip so as to prove the Ouija wrong, thus weening the young people away from its use. Harry's wife was afraid, so she told him of the "message". To her surprise Harry was unconcerned. He said he had already had a vision of the auto accident and of his fatal heart attack. However, he did not fear death so he wasn't going to mention it to his wife. Harry felt he could continue his "calling" out of the body perhaps better than he could "in the body". His wife felt differently and called off the trip.

In this instance, as in so many others, Harry reminds me more of Socrates than does any other person I know anything about. He is, at the least, a force for good.

# CHAPTER V

## BEYOND THE BARRIERS OF EXPLANATION

Perhaps every living person has had some experiences that defy his own rational "explanations" or the explanations of others. Men and women still dream dreams and see visions. We experience disturbing dreams, something seems to wake us in the night, or we feel vague premonitions. Millions of us are consciously -- and perhaps more improtantly, subconsciously -- committed to the "existence" of God and the reality of the spiritual dimension of the world. When crisis or accidents come, it is not unusual for any of us to slip into the language of religious piety, to speak of God's grace and cosmic intervention. The youth who flocked to the Jesus movement with its casting out of demons were not so far from the mainstream of American life.

If millions of ordinary middle Americans are veering sharply towards a form of fundamentalism in religion (as several commentators warn us[1]), it is not surprising that thousands of counter-cultural youth have moved toward the occultic side of the religious spectrum. Even those who shift all the way towards Satanism are on the same wavelength as the masses who have been embracing the old-time religion since the mid 1970's and now claim to be the moral majority. There are those who claim that when one no longer believes in the devil, then disbelief in God is not far behind. Others, including myself, feel that when men can no longer believe in the traditional idea of God, then they are quite able to believe strongly in the devil. I think this is the point Arthur Miller makes in THE CRUCIBLE. I'm sure it is the point Carlos Castaneda makes in his trilogy about Don Juan.

For decades all of us in Western society could say, with the old-time Communist-hunter, "I led three lives". We have all lived the life of the "child", the life of the "ordinary person", with its rational

73

and irrational interests, and the life of the "educated" adult, locked into the various systems of explanations we call "reasonable" and "scientific".

Many of us never notice the discrepancies between these dimensions, at least consciously, but all of us, unconsciously, have felt our inner and social selves pulled apart by the contradictions between them.

The erruption of youthful (and older people's) interest in the occult can be traced fairly directly to the sense of disease and anxiety caused by the channelization of our psychic and physical energy into the several "roles" demanded of us by our society. In a parabolic way we may say that our manner of life provides us all with three thin blankets that are altogether too short and narrow to cover the different areas of our psyches, rather than with one grand quilt that could cover the whole subject that is the self. We pull and tug to cover our rational aspect and our imaginative aspect gets very cold. We attempt to warm up our emotional-imaginative area, and end up standing naked and foolish in the midst of others who are playing it safe with their rational side. For a long time, those who entered the higher educational process tended to accept the systems of rational explanation as "reality", and suppressed or rejected (or better, deflected) the emotional side of themselves. Since the early sixties, and before that for some forerunners like the "beats" and early "hippies", the rational-scientific systems have been increasingly called into question, and the imaginative-emotional aspect of life more highly valued. For some years now the so-called scientific mentality has been under attack and its exponents on the defensive. That this attack is real and the anti-sentiment deep is shown in the closing off of funds for scientific research and the criticism of the space program.

Why have we come to this verbal, conscious, widespread social reaction against rational sysstems of explanation, manipulation and control? I believe it is because the emotional side of our society has been starved, deflected into drunkenness and drugs, and, in general, the joy of living leached out of us by the standards of our society for so long that our inner beings have risen up in revolt. Partially, the rejection of science and linear-print type logic (McLuhan) is but one side of the reassertion of the need for the unity of the self. On another level, the rejection of technology and its scientific basis is a reaction against the use of science to create more and better engines of death for the armies of the world, while polluting the earth, sky and sea with its refuse. Basically, beyond all speculation, the modern temper, with its high value put on sensualism and mystery is a quest to find the one person each of us really is, so that we might live one, whole, single, satisfying life.

## Clouds of Innocence:  The World of the Child[2]

There are a number of ways of looking at the world of the child, from the romantic glorification of it as an age of innocence and lack of worry to the Freudian vision of childhood as a time of many traumas which serve to make one's adult years what they become. Probably the truth lies somewhere between these two extremes. Without buying the romantic notion of childhood as a time of innocence (for ignorance is not the same as innocence), we may state that the child is more of a unitary personality, no matter how immature its structure, than the usual adult in our society. In childhood, the flat distinctions between emotion and reason, between imagination and "reality" have not yet been made. This is reflected in the games of children as well as in the literature of childhood, the fairy tale and pseudo-fairy tale.

Most children have a vague, but real, sense of sacred (or special) space and time. They know that if all times are the same, then no time means anything at all. What could be more boring than a whole summer's vacation full of time to be filled, unless some times were special, like the baseball game or the trip to the beach? Children divide up their time; time for this game, time for that. They retreat from the activity around them, quite often, into their own time and space. The time spent here is not the same time as that spent in other activities, nor is the space just a "space", rather it takes on magical characteristics. In their special place children may secret their treasures -- rocks, dolls, pocket knives -- that have their own power. Children may even talk to their possessions, girls to their dolls, boys to their rocks or cars. As children grow older, conditioned into the internalization of systems of rational thought and codes of moral behavior (called Parent Tapes by Dr. Harris), they gradually lose touch with this "other" "unseen" world. Interestingly, as the young learn more and more "words" about the kingdom of heaven and "spiritual" things (in Sunday School or Catechism Classes) they lose the sense of the basic reality of such a realm by virtue of their social conditioning.

Carlos Castenada had this process of the imprinting of public reality

upon the mind of the child made vividly clear to him when Don Ju
aided him in "stopping the world". Suddenly, he realized the subjecti
ity, the conventionality of the Western view of reality. He "sa
for the first time, and what he "saw" was that reality is great
than our conceptions of before and behind, cause and effect, spa
and time, sensible and insensible.

In our world, up to now, the child has been subtly weened away fro
the world of the imagination. Only those with deep seated traum
have held on to this "subjective" world, as in the case of young mal
who continue the practice of masturbation accompanied with viv
sexual fantasies. Even in such cases, the world of the imaginati
is gutted and killed, since such behavior brings with it the sen
of overwhelming guilt.

In time, the child becomes buried in the psyche, entombed aliv
still hungry and thirsty for life, unsatisfied and unfulfilled. We th
become ordinary adults, at first overcome by the exploding potentia
ties of our bodies, then fascinated by the endless series of possibiliti
that promise satisfaction, sexual, intellectual and material. F
the ordinary adult the world is an amorphous mass, with few cle
lines of differentiation in it. It is like the early stage of a growi
embryo, as yet legs and nose may lie close together. The wor
of the spiritual and the rational-logical world are not sharply unde
stood or precisely defined from each other. Before the education
process has its spiritually enervating and splitting effect, the wor
is a place where anything can happen and often does.

I do not think social commentators have ever taken seriously t
WELTANGSHAUUNG, the worldview of the ordinary person. Th
worldview is relatively stable and is the basis for "middle America
ism", just as it is for the "peasant culture" outlook in Europe
elsewhere. This ordinary view of life is "superstitious" (if we a
being cynical) or "open to the spiritual" (if we are being positiv
as well as being rational". It feeds on both unfounded reports (rumoi
as well as "news". There is a place in its purview for supernatur
salvation and nuclear reactors. To the ordinary person, both religi
and science are equally mysterious, even in a literate culture. H
knows no more about the theory of electricity or nuclear energy th
he knows about the inner workings of the Holy Trinity. His perspecti
is limited because it is private and in this limitation the ordina
man retains the possibility of periodically re-entering the spiritu
realm as well as learning the workings of the internal combustic
engine. Within his limits, he is, as yet, a whole man.

This real, though immature wholeness generally begins to disintegrate upon the introduction of the ordinary person to higher education. This disintegration is not necessarily a deliberately calculated process, not is it a necessarily evil event. Before one can build a straight strong wall, one must break up the earth and lay solid foundations in scars cut in the earth -- both of the world and of the personality. What can become a structure of destruction, a real evil, is the knocking down of the structures of the ordinary person's worldview without a conscious effort to replace the less perfect structure with a more perfect one.

The historic aim of a liberal (or "freeing") education has been to construct such a vision of the world that no longer confines and confuses but frees and unites the inner, total self to the end that it might get into more satisfying and useful relationships with all parts of the person's experience. Modern education has only rarely achieved this liberating synthesis, and it is this inward failure that has precipitated the crisis in education. It is a failure of spirit, not a lack of money that is destroying our schools.

The impact of most modern education, even in religiously supported schools and in theological seminaries, has been of driving wedges between the rational functions and the feeling functions of the person. "Objective" consciousness has been placed in opposition to "subjective" consciousness, with the objective position represented as the only "educated" one, and the form of consciousness to be preferred above all others. After a while, in the arena of the mind as in the arena of the military drill field, one learns to go through the motions of thinking and behaving exactly like everyone else. We have one world-view because that is the worldview we have been told is reality. We expect no other reality, reinforce each other in this single minded vision, and not surprisingly, cannot even recognize the reality of experiences that would call that "objective" worldview into question. The divorce of "mind" and "spirit" is complete. Everyone wins (or loses) and all shall have their prizes. Diplomas are awarded.

In the course of such an education, one learns to distrust and inhibit the emotions, to deflect the directness of physical sensations, to defuse, delay and defer the instinct's thrusts toward gratification. The spiritual dimension is either declared dead or placed in escrow. The subjective, even the experiencial event, is suppressed. The personality becomes misshapen, like the body of a person with injured legs, who walks with the aid of crutches. The top half of the body becomes strong, even over-developed, while the bottom portion withers away. Incidents of wholeness, moments of self-confidence, occasions of joy, come only when one is drugged, drunk or in the retreat of a dreaming sleep. The world, which lies before us in booming, buzzing confusion, a perpetual Mardi Gras of sound and color, shape and line, is "understood" but not fully felt to be "real". The sense of unreality is nature's punishment for partiality in personality development. The world is not so much experienced as a dream as it is seen as the shadow of an image that lies outside our field of vision. The features of the persons we meet lose their scars, stubble and sweat, and become the painted living colors of an enbalmed corpse. We ask simple questions and get simple answers from such a world, while the answers to the questions we have never asked (Who am I?, Where did I come from?, Where am I going?, How shall I live?, What can I hope for?) echo and rebound in an internal static that becomes a garbled message, occasionally, in our dreams.

The time has now come when the person's internal static has created external dissonance as well. Every individual unit of life we can investigate shows the person has found his outer "field" of relationships disturbed by the bad "vibrations" within. The crisis of the person (interiority) becomes the crisis of society (exteriority). There can be no crisis within that is not, at the same time, a crisis without, and visa versa. The internal contradictions conditioned into us by our culture produce such loud sounds of inner mourning that, multipled several million times, it becomes a very heavy counter-cultural song, indeed. That song is a dirge, a weeping, wailing hymn of grief of the death of God; the fall of post-historical culture, the rape of the earth (geosphere and biosphere) and the disintegration of man. During the past two decades we have come to readily accept such Apocalyptic, end-of-the-world hysteria as part of our everyday routine. Such is the depth of our despair and the proof of the insanity of our rational systems of thought: We even find it possible to co-opt the politics of doomsday and make it part of our administration of the world.

## Radical Surgery

Jesus once said, "If your right hand causes you to sin, cut it off and cast it away, lest it cause your whole body to be lost." That is rather radical surgery. I do not necessarily support such an approach, in general, but I must observe that horrendous problems make possible and needful horrendous techniques of cure. The radical cure for the much split-personality of modern man has been homeopathic, that is, a hair of the dog that has bit us. The cold calculation of the rational intellect that destroyed the senses of feeling and imagination for millions is now combatted by the hot, wet formlessness of occultic feeling in our time. Such a counterthrust from the side of mind rooted in the imagination-experience produces an opposite, but equally false, one sided view of human nature. Only the fact that those in the grip of the supernatural occult reaction are demonstrably happier than those closed-in by McLuhan's so-called linear thinking, "the reason trip", makes the religious/occult revival a sign of hope for man. A happy man who cannot tell time can learn to use a watch and be happier still, but a sad man, who can tell time, only becomes sadder when he forgets how to read the face of his watch. Where you start is where you go. The way up and the way down are the same; the beginning and the end are but the two sides of home base.

## Kairos and Competence

The revolution in intellectual and spiritual values has been underway for sometime now. It seems appropriate that we move beyond the ventilation of feeling, the sheer joy of cast off repression, the "fixing" of splits in the psyche by astrology, Transactional Analysis and other arcane sciences, to the integration of reason and imaginal feeling through the will (which is to utter the represented word, discipline). The time, it seems to me, has come to shore up the ruins of intellect, to gentle the firey steed of passion and rehabilitate the structure of law and custom. **The center of an integrated self is not now, nor has it ever been, either intellect or feeling, but will. The first signpost on the road to freedom is the arrow pointing toward self-control. And the second is like unto the first, it is endurance. All else is commentary. Freedom is not a possession, it is a direction.** The power of freedom lies in man's intentionality, which is to say, in the exercise of his will.

Self-Therapy -- with its occult techniques -- has become a cultural fact of our time largely because, in no matter how confusedly a way, it stresses the availability of power and counsels the resolution of the human will. Witchcraft is the art of sharpening and directing the intentionality of the whole person; body, intellect, feeling and social-relatedness, through a strong will. Even in the acceptance of the existence of predestinating powers that lie outside the self -- and society -- there is the trumpeted element of our willing

79

choice between the powers we will ally ourselves with or serve. In the act of submission there is as much need for a strength of will (loyalty) as in the act of the will to power. To say "nevertheless not my will, but thy will be done", is the act of a centered-self that arises from a healthy, functioning will. Behind both the twin hells of rigidity of system or chaos of indiscipline, there lies a failure of nerve, a malfunctioning will. "Whatever your hand finds to do, do it with all your might," is a counsel of endurance and steadfastness of will. John Milton's PARADISE LOST inevitably made Lucifer the hero of the poem because it made the fallen angel a paragon of unconquerable will. Yet that was Milton's mistake, since the Scriptures represent God as the source of steadfast love and covenanted faithfulness. The popular version of Christianity has waivered in its estimation of the will and consequently richly deserves the criticisms of Nietzsche -- that it teaches a slave morality -and a slave mentality. The excesses of Nazism and Existentialism with their worship of the will to power arose as reactions to just this deficiency. Where the exercise of the will is seen to be sinful, only sinners will develop the will, but in the direction of the will to individuality (selfishness) rather than of the will to unity (love). For every error in the central religious tradition there arises a score of equally erroneous reactions. To reject the responsibility of being a willing, enduring self and to worship the deciding, willing function are opposite and equal errors. The thrust of the supernatural interest today is toward a restoration of the healthy use of the will, in order to cancel out the present impasse of personality and society.

**Vital and Vitalizing**

The rise of a supernaturalism of vast proportions in our time should signal everyone that the rational-manipulative worldview is simply not a humanly satisfying one for mankind. The erruption of mystical, occultic and pagan elements into the public consciousness is a declaration that man can only live happily in a world that he experiences as alive, full of life and vital powers, closely connected to the life and forces he senses within himself. If electricity and psychoanalysis dispelled the spirits, good and evil, from the world, the rise of occultism and Neo-Pentecostal Christianity marks their return. One strength of the supernaturalistic (one might almost say, the animistic) worldview, often overlooked, is its **relocation of man, and human life, at the center of the cosmic action,** rather than accepting cold, mathematical physical laws. There is no randomness, no chance; there are no "accidents", in a supernaturalistic vision. All is connected, everything has a cause; for every event there is a purpose; we are guided by powers beyond us, with or without our agreement, in the myth-view of religion. Nothing, no matter how small, is without meaning and significance in this outlook. Everything counts. No sparrow falls to the ground without the knowledge and cooperation of the Divine will. Philosophy, for occultist and fundamentalist believers, is teleological.

Such a world of life, force and purpose is capable of inducing great fear as well as a great feeling of "at homeness". It is very true that occultism and Neo-Pentecostalism reawake racial (archetypical) fears of demons, devils and evil powers. Yet, it must be noted, such a fear is not necessarily unhealthy or uncalled for, nor is it as enervating as the feelings of meaninglessness evoked by a mechanical-chemical view of the universe as the vortex of aimless chance. Evil is a human experience; fear is a human emotion; we only fear that which we feel ourselves related to. Evil spirits are at least thought of as alive, and also imply the existence of their opposite, good spirits. They are not finally so death--creating as mindless entropy and pure chance. One has the option, in supernaturalism, of worshipping the evil spirit, which is not a possibility with the second law of thermodynamics. The universal religious tradition also seems to hold out the possibility of escape from the demons, of redemption and release from evil. For most religions -- and occultic practices -- the existence of evil is not an ultimate fact about the universe.

Religious salvation and occult self-therapy both finally rest upon the faith that the force of good in the cosmos will win the struggle with evil and bring all things into peaceful correlation. The existence of evil does not decrease the warm sense of meaning and belongingness one gets from the belief that he or she is united in a struggle of universal importance. There are real, inner-personal rewards of a constantly self-reinforcing nature entailed in the search today for a philosophy of life that goes "beyond the rational explanation". William James, with his emphasis on a "muscular Christianity" that lines up on the side of good in the struggle with evil, would approve. His more than passing interest in psychic phenomena, especially the possibility of communicating with discarnate spirits, would be titilated also.

# CHAPTER VI

## THE FUTURE OF SELF-THERAPY

### The Crisis of Authority

One of the major myths of the twentieth century is the widespread idea that modern men are completely rational and committed to a "scientific" worldview. The number of people in any community in this century who even understand the logical, scientific outlook is -- and always has been -- small. Modern man is as superstitious as any man in any century has been. "Reason" is not only failing now, it has never been fully in control. The rational explanations put forward by scholars, medical doctors and scientists convince only those who are themselves committed to a view of life that has intellectual depths. And these rational explanations do not even begin to cover irrational fears, deep-seated hostilities, poor interpersonal relations and unconscious prejudices. Most of all, in a period that feels the weakness of every form of authority; rational explanations do not answer our most fearful questions; questions about reason and science itself. Psychology, sociology and logic assume reasons for events that befall them. The ordinary man and woman has as many problems with macrophysics as scientists do with microphysics.

There is still the lingering yearning for mystery in mankind, especially in the young. Young people search for the breakthrough of the twilight zone in their lives, exploring haunted houses, playing at witchcraft, reading their horoscopes. Under the conditions of the academic and governmental credibility gap during the past several decades, it is not surprising that we have a renaissance of interest in the occult today. We live in a period of unsettling anxiety induced by the rapid social changes and far-reaching political events during our lifetimes.

Change, but change towards the ever-more disposable, the ever-more expendable, might be called the sign, par excellence, of our time.

Life is nevertheless only seen as motion, only as quantity, by the materialists today. There is -- and has been -- no real change in the sense of qualitative change -- for decades. More and more, despite Alvin Toffler's straight line mathematical reasoning, technological change does not equal dynamic personal change. Once one begins to think of himself in mechanical terms, the decisive change has been made. People with some human sensibilities left then begin to look for other, alternative ways of life. It seems only natural that the path of the occult would suggest itself to them.

Much of our recent experience as a nation has been with Asia where the occult has remained alive and flourishing for centuries. Much of the content of the present occult movement, from Zen to the I-Ching to Accupuncture, has been imported along with heroin and the war-wrecked survivors of Viet-Nam. Coming into the country at precisely a time when men and women are attempting to bring the elements of themselves together into one whole, the occultic practices of the Orient and the Occident are grasped by millions. Whether they realize it or not, these people are attempting to get into some satisfying relationship with their own unconscious -- and to pull together the fragments of their conscious minds. This grasping after every message that comes along is the reason for the "suspension of disbelief", the utter credulity of millions today, shown in their subscription to Arica, Zen, glossalalia, faith healing and Transcendental Meditation, not to mention Transactional Analysis and assorted group therapies. Therefore, the trend that I have identified as self-therapy represents part of this frantic search for self-fulfillment, for release from anxieties, but more for a unification of the scattered parts of our personalities. Particularly in the occult area people are looking for a meaningful myth-world, a new and fruitful referent for meaning. In this seach for something to guide men and women day by day, modern men have uncovered again the underground stream of experience, wisdom, insight and knowledge that I have called the contrapuntal tradition.[1]

The contrapuntal tradition is that literary, artistic and intellectual nexus in which the seed of new ideas are born from the materials of dreams and legends that have haunted the race from the era of cave dwellings to now. The occult has always been part of this nexus, a thread more or less bright according to the person who finds it. The reason for this is that the contrapuntal tradition is in touch with man's unconscious and through it the primal archetypes (as Jung calls them) are tapped, and the realistic objectivity of the

84

psychic or spiritual dimension is experienced. The power of so many of the new groups, religious. occult, psychological and sociological, rests upon this tapping of the contents and desires of the unconscious mind. Because of this, the contrapuntal tradition is variously called psychic, spiritualistic, pagan, heritical, occult, mystical, Bohemian, hippie, sinful, natural, "far-out" or "freaky", but it nevertheless conveys the power to accomplish change in one's state of consciousness.

The disintegration of the Christian mythic-worldview accomplished by the scientific-materialist mythic-worldview in the twentieth century was followed (in our time) by the swift demise of the scientific WELTANGSHAUUNG. We are living now in the vortex of the debris of these cosmic mythic disintegrations and the search for meaning in Fundamentalism and the occult that mark the North American landscape today is the unconscious response of the human psyche to this frightening (and psychically, i.e., here, consciously, paralyzing) situation. I believe Christianity has the mystical depth to heal the psychically wounded in our time, but Christianity, now as always, sems to be more powerful among those at the extreme ends of the spiritual spectrum. These extreme wings of Christianity I call the grubbers and the dreamers. The grubbers are those people who are earnest workers, very serious, who may be quite ethical but who keep their noses to the grindstones and their eyes on the ground. They are oriented to a religion of immanence to such a degree that they often seem to have lost the transcendental dimension of the faith. Out of the most sensitive ethical spirits of this nature, the civil rights and peace movements were born; highly moral activities that were, however, subject to the criticism of not being very spiritual. In this one-dimensional intense activism, the ethical minded among the Christians are really products of secular Western society. In our society we value the hard working, the concerned, the planners and investors, in short the single minded. The problem with being single minded in this sense is that we are not able to get a handle on the future really nor are we actually tapping the sources of power either in the unconscious or in the spiritual world beyond. Soon the motivation of ethical outrage can tire and we can find ourselves without resources to continue the struggle. It is a reflection of a very noble and major strand in Judeo-Christianity to be ethically oriented but without the mystical dimension, it is incomplete. The almost complete prostration of the religious Civil Rights movement by 1975 is historical proof of this assertion.

For a long time there did not seem to be any dreamers in Christianity anymore. particularly in Protestant churches the ethical dimension and the society-serving functions of religion had seemed to have taken over from the mystical and spiritual   elements altogether. Custom and social activity seem to have supplanted religion with its symbolic traditions and spiritual experiences. Then beginning slowly after the second World War the dreamers began to awake within Christendom again. First the searching for the soul seemed to take its cue from the oriental religions with which the West had come into contact so many times in the global conflict. Later, the trend seemed to be towards a re-evaluation of American Indian religions. With the blossoming of the hippie movement, there was a kind of melding of the desire to become more spiritual, both through chemical and meditative means. Eventually, out of the morass of human despair caused by the drug culture, the Jesus movement arose. The era of the dreamer came in with a vengeance. For some years now the dreamer has been riding higher and higher in the saddle of American religion. The dreamers have pulled the old theosophical trick of bringing everything together into a unity whether it belonged together or not. The dreamers and the moderates who have never agreed to the necessity for Christianity being ethical in social life quickly made an unspoken coalition to turn the American church around so as to remove Christianity from the political arena. Right now, the dreamers are not in control of the largest religious organizations, but their universal mysticism is the controlling philosophy on the religious scene. These dreamers have all the spirituality that the grubbers do not. That is their power and it is undoubtedly the contribution they have to make to twentieth century religion, but it is a spirituality unanchored in history and without the iron rod of prophetic ethics. It is often a pantheism and most assuredly it is a theosophy. It is not anchored in the events recorded in the Old and New Testaments so it is quite open to continual sessions of mass meeting for emotional rejoicing over nothing much and is oriented towards a benign neglect of the needs of others. Richard Nixon was its prophet and Ronald Reagan seems to be its Messiah.

The dreamer is the person who takes the spiritual dimension of religion too seriously just as the grubber is the person who does not take the spiritual dimension seriously enough. What is wanting in both is a balance between the needs of self and the needs of neighbor. On balance, however, it might well be that the grubber is closer to the practical ethicism of the Biblical tradition than the dreamer is. What is clear is that the dreamers of today, for the most part, have prostituted the spiritual dimension in the direction of selfishness, that is as a defense of a status quo, do-nothing policy in religion and society. As long as this is the case, few, if any real gains will be made for Christianity, and the occult, because it shares so many features with the dreamers' variety of Christianity, will remain a viable option for many.

The prognosis for the future is not good for institutional Christianity if it remains unable to make itself available to the mass of average people with human problems. Either we discover the mystical depths of Christian faith and show them publically, or we surrender our stake in the people's real religion and become the state-religion of the ruling class -- a situation that history has seen many times before.

## The Great Divorce

In a sense, the Christian establishment has sold out the yearning members of the altered consciousness movement (or counter-culture), while at the same time pandering to the worst instincts of reactionaries of all ages in America. The selfish and the dreamers together inundated the people of the United States in the seventies and eighties, seeking to turn away from the real psychic and physical problems of our times to a nostalgic reverie on middle America. To do this, the teeth of the activistic grubbers in the counter-culture had to be broken by force and money. Both weapons were used, indiscriminately. Because of the moralism of middle America, the reactionary political administration came under serious fire. The corruption of spying and bought political favors rose up to haunt the pseudo-Puritan, Richard Nixon. The callous cruelty of the media-appointed high priest of Americanism as a religion, Billy Graham, brought him to shame in his own press. The disgust and despair of the millions, both in the youthful counter-culture and among older middle Americans rose like a muddy tide. Men and women of every place and of all ages felt that we came to the very edge of our civilized world. To go much further was to run the risk of falling off. Nixon had to go. There was a renewed retreat into quietistic privatism. We wanted to retreat to some small, quiet certainties of the home, school, family and community. We wanted to tune out the maddened world, to reduce the number of shouting voices and get things under control by getting control of the stimuli that distract us. We wanted to filter out the demands and pleas of the world around us so as to be able to manage our own minds and our own lives again. Older people may say they want to get back to basics, but youth will only say they want to get themselves "together". Both generations really want the same things. The return to conservatism by youth in the 1980's illustrates the truth of this observation.

## Healing Power

**Life is hard.** If there were to be any standard motto for tombstones, it should be those three simple words. The vast web of technological, mechanical slaves our culture has devised to shield us from the seriousness and the risk of the world cannot hide that truth from one who lives very long. Every Scripture, every poet, every playwright, and novelist worth the name teaches us the difficulty of becoming and remaining a human being in the world. Men and women bear the brunt not only of the blows of chance and of nature but, most of all, the cruelties and unconcern of one another. Mankind, unlike any other species, is harder on itself than is its environment or any natural enemy. We come to birth in blood and grow into our individual identities in trauma. Adulthood leaves scars as wll as successes on our psyches and our bodies. The philosophical concepts of good and evil, said by both occultism and religion to be in struggle in the universe, are less abstractions of thought than they are mythological personifications of the ambiguous conflicts within every personality and between every person and his fellowman. The yearning for healing is great, now, in our time, but it has always been so. The ancient caves of France and India were not painted, nor the pyramids raised, nor the words of the prophets recorded because man was at peace with himself. Just the opposite -- man has always felt split, between the mind and the heart, the body and the spirit, the good and the evil. Therefore, mankind has always sought healing, wholeness -unity of the self with itself -- and with the beyond in our midst.

The following are only a few of the ways in which we are groping today to find this wholeness. There are no signs that the quest is diminishing.

## Harry's Help

Peter Evans (a pseudonym) is a young instructor in literature. His life, until recently has been marked by quiet despair, a deep sense of guilt and a sense of no way out. That was before Peter met Harry. I introduced Harry in the last chapter, the psychic who uses his abilities to gain men's attention so that he may tell them about Christ.

Harry would seem like a very poor hero or major character for any story. However, he is just far enough fetched to be real and effective in today's searching world. Harry is an executive in a large company and old enough to be the father of most of the people he meets plying his Socratic trade. He dresses conservatively, although like Socrates he is usually rumpled and is always talking. His church background is Southern Baptist and in his manner and conversation he seems warmly evangelical. However, his technique and perhaps some of his philosophy certainly diverges from conservative tenets. He seems a mixture of Baptist street corner evangelist and Carlos Castenada's Don Juan.

Harry's similarities to Socrates are more than just surface. He spends almost all his time now visiting in University areas, talking to students and their young instructors. He is very effective in these encounters. One would think that college made people sophisticated in ways that would prevent their being affected by people like Harry, and perhaps at one time that was true. It is no longer true in this spiritually searching age. From my visits to the mid-Western city where Harry resides, I would say that he is perhaps the most effective worker with young people that I have ever seen. I believe this is the case because Harry offers not only counsel but healing and a deep spiritual inspiration. This is what men and women are looking for today.

The search for healing is the modern version of the ancient quest, recounted in myths and legends, enshrined in our dreams. The quest is the drive of the life force within each one of us to become fully human -- to actualize the full potential that is born within us. What are our problems and hangups, but blocks to our self-actualization? Who are our enemies if not immature parts of our own selves? The search for healing is the unconscious urge to reunite the unconscious and the conscious minds, to make the stuff of dreams and the items of reality one.

Harry is the improbable counter-cultural hero of today's spiritual search because he represents a living combination of traditional religious attitudes and an openness to what we have traditionally thought of as occultic. He takes seriously the reality of spirits and demons, is himself a practicing psychic, and is at ease in the informal relationships and cult language of astrology that forms so much of the referencial speech of the young. Harry seems like a person programmed to seek out and zero in on spiritual needs. Like Socrates he will strike up conversations with complete strangers and take advantage of the peculiarities of his personality. Harry has a natural ability to "read minds", which he utilizes to attract people's attention and to close in on them with his "preaching". In the case of Peter Evans, he sensed the distress in the man and brought about a profound conversion which appears to have made both Peter and his wife very happy. While this may seem like somewhat ordinary evangelism, as we tell it, it is hardly that in the experience. Harry introduced Peter and along with him, Peter's wife, and another professor, Jim and Jim's wife, to a world where spirits and spiritual things are more real than the concrete events of everyday. Through these four young adults Harry's circle is now reaching the students in the city university where they teach. A spiritual group has sprung up in the home of one of them that has attracted students who have not been going to church and in some cases have been mixed up in the more negative aspects of the occult.

## Occult Ideas in American Christianity

Occult ideas are as old as Western civilization, but with the exception of a small fringe of Protestantism that has formed the Spiritualist churches, occultic ideas, in the main, have been excluded from Christianity. One of the salient features of the occult revolution in recent years has been the introduction of Spiritualist and occultic ideas into the framework and beliefs of nominal Christians. As Harry represents the introduction of some of these into the Christianity that is now passing into the lives of his university friends, we must come to grips with these increasingly influencial thought forms. Perhaps the most interesting and completely different "doctrine" to be adopted by many otherwise orthodox Christians today is the concept of **reincarnation.** Reincarnation is one of the oldest religious ideas of mankind. It involves the belief that the soul is immortal and that it passes from life to life. The great philosopher, Plato, believed in reincarnation, and has reincarnational motifs expressed through the mouth of Socrates in several dialogues. Ancient Greek reincarnation theories included not only the belief that human beings who died might come back as other human beings, but apparently also held that men might return as animals since Socrates suggested that philosophers who soared away into the abstract might come back as soaring birds.

How much the ancient Greek belief in reincarnation was connected to the Hindu belief in Karma we do not know. In all events Hinduism seems to be solidly based upon a belief in Karma or the doctrine

90

that the soul is absolutely immortal and transmigrates from life to life both through human and animal lives in response to the goodness or evil of one's present life. In India among the Hindus, Jains and Buddhists, there is no doubt whatsoever of the reality of reincarnation.

In the West, reincarnational ideas have been known, to be sure, from times of ancient Greece, however, the doctrine of Karma and the transmigration of the soul form no part of Christian theology and have always been resisted by orthodox theologians. Perhaps it is felt that the doctrine of reincarnation depreciates the worth of the physical life and calls in question the salvation which Jesus Christ is said to have accomplished for man by His death and resurrection. It is difficult to see how a doctrine of reincarnation can fit in with the Christian emphasis.

With all the difficulties of bringing together any basic Western Christian belief with a basic Eastern religious belief, there seem to be many people willing to make the attempt at synthesis today. For example, there is the Christ-Light community of Deming, New Mexico. This organization sponsors The New Age Church of Truth, that mingle together elements of Neo-Pentecostalism and Spiritualism. Some of the lectures advertised by representatives of The New Age Church of Truth include, "The Holy Spirit: Baptism, Gifts and Powers"; and "The Human Aura; and Finer Forces of Man". Others advertise special healing services, "The Invisible World and Its Mysteries" and "Be Your Own Prophet!" I would suggest that this strange amalgam of Christianity and occultism is just the kind of other-worldly mixture that many people of all ages today are looking for. For a variety of reasons I will simply subsume under the rubric of a crisis of authority, men and women today are not drawn by the moral and social sensitivity of Christian theology nor by the rationality of doctrinal presentation and are actually turned off by clergymen who present these high points of Christian development. To the contrary, people seem drawn to the weird, the unusual, the emotionally charged and above all, to the personally participatory. While traditional Christianity contains much that invites every individual to full participation in its thought, activity and organization, these new spiritual seekers do not find the elements of rationality and responsibility attractive. Perhaps the turning to an individual emphasis in the personal experience of speaking in tongues, being healed of emotional and physical disabilities, having their future lives charted and other such activities represent the counter-cultural desire to reject the myth of objective consciousness. People want to feel,

91

not know; they want to be part of, not hold membership in; they do not want to be reminded of the needs and problems of others, but they want assistence with their own individual needs. Stated starkly like this, the selfishness and something of the immaturity of this way of looking at things becomes clear. It may be much clearer, then, as to why the doctrine of reincarnation, with its comforting promise that this highly valued individual self will not come to a termination even at death, is so appealing now for millions.

If one can persuade oneself that there is enough indication of the survival of the soul after death then a great many problems that plague life fall away. It is in search of such evidences of survival that literally millions of North Americans now go. Recently an expert in the area of occultism estimated that reincarnation forms part of the belief system of some twenty million people in America. While this may be an exaggeration, it is certainly not an exaggeration to suggest that the number of people interested in reincarnation is quite high. More recent surveys would corraborate the belief that reincarnation is very popular in America. The large number of books bearing on reincarnation and attempts to establish it on a firm basis would tend to bear out the large population vitally interested in this belief. Quite recently, the popular writer, Jess Stearn, made a significant contribution to this literature in the THE SEARCH FOR A SOUL, TAYLOR CALDWELL'S PSYCHIC LIVES.

**Hypnotic Regression**

Jess Stearn[2] writes of the search for some "evidence" of the survival of human personality after death, and of further "proof" of reincarnation through the process of hypnosis which is used to "regress" a person (in this case, the novelist, Taylor Caldwell) backwards in their life to birth and before that (according to Stearn's belief) into previous lives. According to Stearn's account, Ms. Caldwell did not consciously believe in reincarnation, but under hypnotic regression she spoke not only of one, but of thirty-seven previous lives. Her "lives" ranged from one that ended only two years before her present birth to an existence in Biblical times when she was the mother of Mary Magdalene.[3] Stearn seems convinced that this "research" and other investigations he has carried out and reported elsewhere[4] prove the reality of reincarnation. Ms. Caldwell, in an epilogue to the book, declares that she still does not believe in survival.[5]

Hypnotic regression is not new. Something like the technique Stearn employed with Ms. Caldwell has been used before (including an early use by Jess Stearn) to "regress" people to what is claimed to be a life before the present one. What does it prove? Whan can it possibly prove? Certainly not reincarnation -- or not reincarnation alone. Even if one ruled out trickery or fraud, there are several alternative hypotheses that could account for the eruption of such strange material from hypnotized minds.

First, other "supernatural" or "spiritual" hypotheses are possible. The reported experiences may be the result of spirit "possession", i.e., of being invaded by a discarnate spirit or spirits, something like the supposed possession of a Spiritualist medium in a trance. Secondly, psychological hypotheses are possible, including multiple personality or schizophrenia. The experience of hypnosis may remove the compensating "censor" of the conscious mind and allow these less well-developed "personalities" to emerge. Thirdly, the uninhibited unconscious (under hypnosis) may simply fantasize, spinning engaging tales out of materials it has acquired through reading, movies, plays and television.

Fourthly, the material presented under hypnosis may be due to an increased extrasensory perception talent stimulated by the hypnotic state. Just where this "material" would be drawn from is another question.

Many people interested in the occult are now dabbling in hypnotic regression. I recently had a case of such regression reported by me by university students. A girl student was "regressed" after being hypnotized. She reported events in her life one year before, five years before, ten, fifteen and twenty years before (the last being the year when she was born). Then the hypnotist asked her where she was and who she was, twenty-five years ago. Suddenly she answered in a deep voice, "I'm in a convent. My name is Sister Luke. I am forty-seven years old." This event caused great excitement among the group. It was followed by questions from the hypnotist. Everyone present was impressed, although the "subject" once awakened, claimed to remember nothing.

Several days later the young lady apologetically reported to the group that she had been faking during the whole hypnotic session. I do not know what the case is in the matter of Jess Stearn and Taylor Caldwell, but I do know that the above story of supposed "hypnotic regression" is true. I spoke to ten people who were witness to the whole affair.

## By the Power of Dreams

Recently a young man (a junior in a small college in a northern state) sat in my study and told me of his suffering adventures since his senior year at a large city high school. He was dressed neatly enough in the blue jean trousers and jacket of the contemporary college student. His hair was moderately long and wavy, as was his beard and moustache. His story was familiar in its general outline to anyone who has worked closely with a college community over the last two decades. This young man had experimented with every kind of herb and drug. He had "done chemicals" (in the youth of argot) ranging from LSD-25 to mescaline. He had "smoked dope" (marijuana) frequently. At examination time he had tried "speed" (amphetamines). Towards the end of his experimental period (for he was not "off drugs"), he had become involved with drug users of a violent disposition, who were "into" "Black occultism." Their references to Satan, their fascination with guns and knives had frightened him -- quite sensibly frightened him, I think. He began to think of Jesus Christ and release one morning after having the following dream.

## The Seventh Tide: Through Death to Birth

The young man fixed me with an anxious look. "Should I be talking about this?" he asked. "Of course, if you talk about it now and forget about it," I answered. "O.K., but I get upset thinking about this." "Just don't get compulsive and think about it all the time," I rejoined.

"Well, I was smoking dope," he began, "and got pretty well 'wrecked' (i.e., intoxicated) before I fell into a trance, or sleep, I'm not sure which. Anyway, I had this dream, or this vision, or this vision-in-a-dream. It was scary and comforting at the same time.

"In my dream, I was under water, I was floating in and out with the tide. As I would float closer into shore, I could look down and see the clean sand below me. I could look up and see the sun's rays penetrating through the water towards me. As I approached the beach, the floor of the sea gently tilted up to meet the sandy edge, which was the boundary of the ocean. The closer I came to the shore, the warmer the water became. It was quite warm and pleasant."

"But I also floated back out, seaward. I could feel a definite pull, a kind of tidal motion. This tide made me float away from the warm water to deeper water where it was colder. At times, I would feel as if I was going farther and farther out. Then I was in really deep water, so deep I could look up through many, many varied colors of water and sunlight mingled together. Once, after floating into where it was warm, I was pulled further out than ever. I looked up and I saw a boat floating on the ocean's surface far above me. I sort of woke up and cried out, 'What is the name of this dream?' Then I saw, as it were, a television set with the words, 'The Seventh Tide' displayed upon its screen. At that moment I knew that the boat was Jesus, the fisherman. He was fishing for me."

I talked with this young man for some times and was surprised to find that he had not associated his well-developed dream with the myths and symbols of death and rebirth. The sea, the fountain of life, figured in it. The warm water with the strong in and out pull of the tides fairly cried out that they represented the womb and the birth process. But it was when I mentioned Paul's imagery of dying with Christ in the water of Baptism and being resurrected with Him as we come up out of the water that I got my biggest surprise. He claimed never to have read anything in the Bible, yet he was "following Jesus". He fairly trembled with joy when I gave him a New Testament. Here was one of the "Jesus people" of the purest sort. He had started "following Jesus" (his words) without benefit of the church, the campus religious programs, the clergy, or even of the New Testament. I could not stifle the exclamation, "Out of the mouth of babes thou has perfect praise", or a further, "Yet wisdom is justified by all her children."

I think Jesus would have loved this boy who threw over four years of drug abuse on the strength of a vision in a drug-induced dream, without fully understanding it. He saw in it one thing needful (Jesus Christ), and he saw what I did not see (Jesus as the boat) when I heard the vision recounted. Jesus would have loved this boy, but I'm not sure that the Christian church is ready for him.

### Future Prospects: Neo-Pentecostalism and Occultism

A period of history which deeply searches for participation and a personal experience of the reality of the spiritual world, must be expected to run beyond the bounds of traditional thoelogy and normal church behavior. Just what deep psychological needs are being met by the response of thousands of people to Charismatic and Pentecostal type meetings is difficult to say. We immediately think of a search for security, perhaps occasioned by the country-wide sense that the nation had become unglued and that not only national unity but national sanity and morality were coming apart. Certainly the escalation of the struggle between the various partisan groups concerning the Vietnam war, the full participation of minority groups in civic affairs and the spread of drug abuse to all quarters of the country, tended to give some validity to the idea that the nation was in deep trouble during the 1960's and in the early 1970's. Perhaps only a minority of people on the North American continent ever gave themselves over to a serious commitment to social change, so the rise of violence and serious cleavages within the population was enough to frighten most people back to a very old-fashioned Protestant version of religion in which the faith was sought for purely individual and personal reasons. An any rate, by 1975 and continuing through the 1980's, that is what happened.

On a positive note, we may look at the return to mysticism, including occultism and Neo-Pentecostalism, as a serious return to the vertical dimension in religion, the emphasis upon the spiritual that had been lacking during the years of social protest. We may also see this movement in terms of a positive response to a well-taken feeling of fright at what we were doing to ourselves as human beings. The life of the spirit, of the imagination; of the individual's need to face up to his own mortality had been neglected and now must have its due.

John Stevens Kerr,[6] writing about the Jesus people, has this to say about one of the institutions founded for young former drug users. The constant reinforcement of each other's commitment to the new way of looking at the world which Kerr reports is similar in psychological structure to sectarian groups both occultic and religious.

"The program at Renewal House, is Jesus. The premise is that if you let Jesus save you, all your other problems can be worked out."

"The daily program squeezes in a half-hour of prayer, two and one-half hours of Bible study (poster in room: "Read the Bible -- it'll scare the hell out of you") and an evening of witnessing and testimony. In addition there are work details and 'productivity time' for crafts, reading, personal development."

"But that doesn't tell the whole story. Renewal House is like a 24-hour Bible study. Jesus and the wonderful things he does make up the whole conversation, whether washing dishes (wearing a 'Jesus is Divine Love' T-shirt) or making candles."

"The residents have left their drugs behind. They've found the Ultimate High: 'When the Lord comes in you, you're addicted enough!'"

"Those over-thirty people who equate a conversion atmosphere with sobriety have missed out on the Jesus people style. If the Bible study lacks the scholarly depth of a seminary classroom, it also misses the academic monotony. The leader goes verse by verse, sticking to the positive promises of God, which evoke some sure-fire 'Praise the Lord's'."

"'I wonder how Satan feels when we are praising the Lord here?' asks the leader, Bob Carsten of Lutheran Youth Alive. The group in the living room laughs out loud. 'The dude is shook up!' one resident gleefully announces. 'Praise the Lord!' 'Praise to Jesus!' 'Jesus, Lord!' When the study is over, they join in a circle doing a Greek-style dance as they sing 'It's bubbling in my soul.'"

"They leave, embracing each other, talking about how great Jesus is, telling each other that they are going to make it with Jesus along. Over the doorway as they go out hangs a poster. It reads: 'Love is the awesome discovery of Christ in another person, a friend.'"

There is no doubt that the rather fraternity style, surface[6] Christianity portrayed here is a great improvement over the lostness that many youths have felt over the last decade, yet it is hardly a mature faith, for it remains to be seen how it will stand up to the pressures of life outside a community house, or how it will muster the intellectual power to deal with moral issues in society. One wonders what "Jesus people" think about the tangled moral issues of abortion and the life-challenging problems of disarmament and the multiplication of nuclear weapons.

In the search for individual healing, however, we may have to agree that the psychic wounds of our people are so deep that they need to be dealt with on an individual basis before we can return again to problems of national and international scope. While taking such a positive line towards both the Jesus people with their Pentecostal proclivities as well as towards the individuality of occultic movements, we must not forget that both trends are at best distorted forms of religion that lack the depth required to effect genuine healing.

Their major danger is atomism, an emphasis upon the particular individual which de-emphasizes the context of community life in which we all are found. Majoring in such a particularistic fashion is like treating individual sufferers with typhoid fever and ignoring the epidemic that is searing its way through the body politic.

## A Final Warning

While I expect people to continue to stress reincarnation, to engage in hypnotic regression, to consult their dreams and visions, as well as the Tarot cards, and horoscopes and to seek enlightenment even through "readings" made from personal objects, or from the auras that they will strain to make out around their heads, I must put forward some warnings that I hope are taken seriously.

I do not want to belabor the obvious fact of the personal and communal short-comings of all forms of mystical, individualistic religion, or to stress again the wide divergency of occultic doctrine from the traditional theology of Judaism and Christianity. These things are obvious, at least after they have been pointed out. What I do want to stress is the grave weakness that all sectarian movements share and which has brought trouble on the world over and over again. This is the dependency of mystical, individual participatory groups upon charismatic leadership for their foundation, development and survival. It may not seem so frightening the the Neo-Pentecostal and occultic groups which are growing so quickly today are in fact dependent upon charismatic individuals until we remember Hitler with his hypnotic voice and obsessive ideas or Charles Manson and his group of youthful followers who came to call him "God". Scarcely less scandulous behavior than Manson's can be observed on the new religious and occultic fronts if one opens his eyes. A television healer-preacher, who was under indictment in federal and state courts for the misuse of funds, went on scores of stations, appealing to the same public he had received support from asking for further funds to bail himself out of his predicament. Going beyond this, the same man sent letters around asking people to borrow money to contribute to his needs, without bothering to even say why he needed the funds. It seems beyond reason that the pbulic should continue to support someone whose activities were so decisively called into question, and yet this is what we find over and over. For the charismatic leader, denunciation seems only to increase his power over the true believers. This is the secret -- and tragedy -- of Jonestown and the Rev. Jim Jones.

The charismatic person, as a type, is nonmoral. He may be either good or evil, but he is always spiritual in the serious and impressive way that attracts and holds followers. The charismatic person may be ethical or immoral or amoral. This is the philosophical, the theological explanation for a Hitler, a Wallace, a Kennedy, a King, a Schweitzer, a John XXIII, a John Paul II, a Jim Jones, and a Rev. Moon.

Perhaps all organizations depend upon elements of the charismatic for their direction and inspiration, however, emotional participatory groups are much more dependent upon the inspring leader than are well organized groups with a recognized order of authority. This makes them subject to wild swings in temper and direction, depending upon the whims of the leader. Herein lies the danger to the individual who commits himself to such a group or comes to such a charismatic figure for counseling and help. In political terms we might say such a group lacks an adequate system of checks and balances on authority. While many wholesome personalities may come forward in such mystical, emotional movements, there is always a high risk of the unethical leader leading his followers into destructive paths.

To have charisma means to be attractive in the deepest human meaning of that term. It means to be fascinating in the deep sense the Rudolph Otto identified in describing the holy and the demonic as being fascinating and attractive. In terms of the present youth culture, it means to be a "heavy" personality. Basically, to be charismatic means that one bears a spirit. This may be the good spirit but it may also be the ambiguous spirit of nationalism; the selfish spirit of sectarianism or party loyalty; or even the immoral spirit of sensuality or depravity. In a time when even within the confines of traditional Christianity, the charismatic is being stressed, while among the great legion outside the church the mysterious and the occult are being tapped as sources of comfort, security, and healing, we need to exercise the ability to discern the different kinds of spirits lest we be led astray.

# FOOTNOTES

## CHAPTER I

1. John Charles Cooper, RELIGION IN THE AGE OF AQUARIUS (The Westminster Press, 1971).

2. See Paul H. Kocher, THE OCCULT SCIENCES IN THE RENAISSANCE (University of California Press, 1972).

3. See Carl Gustav Jung, MEMORIES, DREAMS, REFLECTIONS, Recorded and edited by Aniela Jaffe (Trans. by Richard and Clara Winston, Vintage Books, New York, 1963); pp. 155-156.

4. Norman Mailer, THE ARMIES OF THE NIGHT (The New American Library, 1968).

5. Information taken from personal communication to the author. Source protected.

6. Information taken by a selection from the cassette tape, "Dallas '72", a report of the meeting of the American Psychiatric Association produced by Smith Kline and French. Dr. Mansel Pattison's address is entitled "Witchcraft, Rootwork, Faith Healing and Psychiatry".

7. News release from Temple University, Philadelphia, Pennsylvania, dated June 17, 1970.

8. **Ibid.**

9. Georg Ivanovich Gurdjieff, in THE MORNING OF THE MAGICIANS, quoted in THE CHILDREN OF CHANGE by Don Fabun (Glencoe Press, 1979); p. 36.

10. Jean Paul Sartre, BEING AND NOTHINGNESS (trans. by Hazel E. Barnes, Philosophical Library, New York, 1956); "Bad Faith"; II, pp. 55-58.

11. **Ibid.**

12. Ralph Woods, O.P., "Occultism: Countercultural Religion", in LISTENING, Spring, 1971; Vol. 6, No. 2; p. 119, (Published by the Schools of Theology in Dubuque, Iowa.)

13. Cooper, **op. cit.**


## CHAPTER II

1. See Donald Nugent, "The Renaissance and/or Witchcraft", in CHURCH HISTORY, March, 1971, Vol. XXXX, No. 1.

2. **Ibid.**

3. **Ibid.**

4. Nat Freedland, THE OCCULT EXPLOSION (G. P. Putnam's Sons, 1972).

5. Peter Rowley, NEW GODS IN AMERICA (David McKay Co., Inc., 1971).

6. Hal Lindsey, SATAN IS ALIVE AND WELL ON PLANET EARTH (Zondervan Publishing House, 1972).

7. Anya Seton, GREEN DARKNESS (Houghton-Mifflin Co., 1972).

8. Leonard Wolf, A DREAM OF DRACULA, IN SEARCH OF THE LIVING DEAD, (Little Brown, 1972).

9. Raymond McNally and Radu Florescu, IN SEARCH OF DRACULA: A TRUE HISTORY OF DRACULA AND VAMPIRE LEGENDS (New York Graphic, 1972).

10. William Peter Blatty, THE EXORCIST (Harper & Row, 1971).

11. Thomas Tryon, THE OTHER (Alfred A. Knoph, 1971).

12. Carlos Castaneda, THE TEACHINGS OF DON JUAN, A YAQUI WAY OF KNOWLEDGE (University of California Press, 1968).

13. Carlos Castaneda, A SEPARATE REALITY, FURTHER CONVERSATIONS WITH DON JUAN (Simon and Schuster, 1971).

14. Carlos Castaneda, JOURNEY TO IXTLAN (Simon and Schuster, 1972).

15. Richard Bach, JONATHAN LIVINGSTON SEAGULL -- A STORY (The Macmillan Co., 1970).

16. Erich Von Daniken, GODS FROM OUTER SPACE (Bantam Books, 1972).

17. Erich Von Daniken, CHARIOTS OF THE GODS? (Bantam Books, 1971).

18. See Astrology ad inserted between pp. 58-59 of PLAYBOY, April 1973, Vol. 20. No. 4.

19. THE COMPLETE CONCORDANCE TO THE REVISED STANDARD VERSION BIBLE.

20. Information from personal communication to the author. Source protected.

21. See Daniel Yankelovich, "The New Naturalism", in THE SATURDAY REVIEW, April 1, 1972; pp. 32ff. Also see FINDING A SIMPLER LIFE, John C. Cooper (United Church Press, 1974), and THE JOY OF THE PLAIN LIFE, John C. Cooper (Zondervan, 1982).

22. **Ibid.**, p. 35.

23. **Ibid.**

24. See SELECTED WRITINGS OF ST. THOMAS AQUINAS, (Bobbs-Merrill, Library of Liberal Arts, Indianapolis, Indiana, 1965); p. 94.

25. See David Ross, ARISTOTLE (London, 1960); pp. 95-99; 107-108. See also Aristotle, GENERATION AND CORRUPTION, II, 10, 33b, 16-20.

26. Hal Lindsey, **op. cit.**

27. Exerpted from a student term paper. Source protected.

28. Robert Heinlein, STRANGER IN A STRANGE LAND (Berkley Medallion Books, 1961).


## CHAPTER III

1. Material taken from a student term paper. Source protected.

2. Dennis Wheatley, THE DEVIL AND ALL HIS WORKS (American Heritage Press, New York, 1971); pp. 10-11.

3. G.F.W. Hegel, THE PHENOMENOLOGY OF MIND (Trans. by Sir James Baillie, Humanities Press, 1964); pp. 338ff.

4. Wheatley, **op. cit.**

5. Maurice Bessy, A PICTORAL HISTORY OF MAGIC AND THE SUPERNATURAL (Spring Books,   printed in Czechoslovákia by Svoboda, Prague, 1968).

6. Mircea Eliade, MYTHS, DREAMS AND MYSTERIES (Harper Torchbooks, New York, 1960).

7. See "Mana" in the Encyclopedia Britannica, Inc., (William Benton, Publisher, Chicago, 1966), Vol 14, pp. 746-747. Basically, Mana means power beyond the ordinary, or of supernatural origin.

8. Daniel Yankelovich, "The New Naturalism", THE SATURDAY REVIEW, **op. cit.**

9. **Ibid.**

10. See Jung, **op.cit.**, p. 221. Jung wrote a paper, "Synchronicity: An Acausal Connecting Principle", which is published in Volume 8 of his COLLECTED WORKS.

11. See Leibnitz, "The Monadology", pp. 199-214 in MODERN CLASSICAL PHILOSOPHERS, Edited by Benjamin Rand (Houghton-Mifflin, Co., second edition, 1952).

12. See Sybil Leek, THE SYBIL LEEK BOOK OF FORTUNE TELLING (The Macmillan Co., 1969).

13. See Carlos Castaneda's three books on the teachings of Don Juan, **op.cit.**

14. See my discussion of Reincarnation below.

15. Plato, THE PHAEDO, in PLATO (Trans. by B. Jowett, Walter J. Black, Inc., Roslyn, NY, 1942); p. 111.

16. See Ian Stevenson, M.D., TWENTY CASES SUGGESTIVE OF REINCARNATION (American Society for Psychical Research, NY, 1966; The Proceedings of the American Society for Psychical Research, Vol. XXVI, September, 1966).

## CHAPTER IV

1. See J. Schoneberg Setzer, "The God of Ambrose Worall and of Edgar Cayce" in RELIGION IN LIFE, Autumn, 1972, Vol. XLI, No. 3; pp. 390-409.

2. **Ibid.**

3. **Ibid.**

4. See Rudolph Otto, THE IDEA OF THE HOLY (trans. by John W. Harvey, Oxford University Press, 1946).

5. See "Glossalalia -- No Language but a Cry" in PSYCHOLOGY TODAY, August, 1972, Vol. 6, No. 3, pp. 48ff; and William J. Samarin, TONGUES OF MEN AND ANGELS (The Macmillan Co., 1972).

6. Plato, THE APOLOGY, in PLATO, **op. cit.**

7. Oscar Bagnall, THE ORIGINS AND PROPERTIES OF THE HUMAN AURA (University Books, NY, 1970, New Revised Edition.)

8. See Carlos Casteneda's three books on Don Juan, **op. cit.**

9. C.P. Snow, THE TWO CULTURES AND THE SCIENTIFIC REVOLUTION (Cambridge University Press, NY, 1963).

10. See Douglass McFerran, "The New Magic" in COMMONWEAL, September 19, 1971, Vol. XCIV, No. 20; pp. 477-480.

11. Eliade. **op. cit.**

12. See Hellmut Wilhelm, CHANGE: EIGHT LECTURES ON THE I-CHING (Harper Torchbooks, 1964).

13. Westminster Press, Philadelphia, 1971.

14. Personalized horoscope prepared for me by the Time Pattern Research Institute, Valley Stream, NY.


## CHAPTER V

1. Lowel D. Streiker and Gerald S. Strober, RELIGION AND THE NEW MAJORITY (Association Press, 1972); and Dean M. Kelley, WHY CONSERVATIVE CHURCHES ARE GROWING (Harper and Row, 1972).

2. This discussion of the quest for the unity of the self was first delivered as a public lecture at the University of Evansville, Evansville, Indiana, in April, 1973).


## CHAPTER VI

1. See John C. Cooper, THE ROOTS OF THE RADICAL THEOLOGY, **op. cit.**

2. Jess Stearn, THE SEARCH FOR A SOUL, TAYLOR CALDWELL'S PSYCHIC LIVES (Doubleday & Co., Inc., 1973).

3. **Ibid.**

4. Jess Stearn, THE SEARCH FOR THE GIRL WITH THE GREEN EYES, A VENTURE INTO REINCARNATION, (Doubleday & Co., Inc., 1968). And Jess Stearn, YOGA, YOUTH AND REINCARNATION (Doubleday & Co., Inc., 1965).

5. Stearn, THE SEARCH FOR A SOUL, **op. cit.**, pp. 309-321.

6. John S. Kerr, "The Bible Turns Them On" in THE LUTHERAN, February 7, 1973, Vol. II. No. 3, pp. 7-8.

# SELECTED BIBLIOGRAPHY OF OCCULT BOOKS

**Note:** ***most important; **well worth reading;
*could leave till later.

## I. BOOKS BY OCCULTISTS

** Crowley, Aleister. MAGIC IN THEORY AND PRACTICE. Castle Books, n.d.

** LaVey, Anton. THE SATANIC BIBLE. Avon pbk., 1969.

** Leek, Sybil. THE COMPLETE ART OF WITCHCRAFT. Signet pbk., 1973.

## II. HISTORIES AND STUDIES OF THE OCCULT

*** Cavendish, Richard. THE BLACK ARTS. Capricorn pbk., 1967.

*** Clarens, Carlos. AN ILLUSTRATED HISTORY OF THE HORROR FILM. Capricorn pbk., 1968.

* Freedland, Nat. THE OCCULT EXPLOSION. Berkley pbk., 1972.

** Haining, Peter. WITCHCRAFT AND BLACK MAGIC. Bantam pbk., 1972.

* Holzer, Hans. GHOST HUNTER. Ace pbk., 1972.

*** Kerr, Howard. MEDIUMS, AND SPIRIT-RAPPERS, AND ROARING RADICALS. University of Illinois Press, 1972.

*** Lovecraft, Howard Phillips. SUPERNATURAL HORROR IN LITERATURE. Dover pbk., 1972.

\*\*\*    Malinowski, Bronislaw. MAGIC, SCIENCE AND RELIGION. Double Anchor pbk., 1954.

\*\*\*    McNally, Raymond T., and Radu Florescu. IN SEARCH OF DRACULA. Warner pbk., 1973.

\*\*\*    Ostrander, Sheila, and Schroeder, L. PSYCHIC DISCOVERIES BEHIND THE IRON CURTAIN, Bantam pbk., 1973.

\*    Seth, Ronald. IN THE NAME OF THE DEVIL. Tower pbk., 1969.

\*\*\*    Summers, Montague, ed. THE MALLEUS MALEFICARUM OF HEINRICH KRAMER AND JAMES SPRENGER. Dover pbk., 1971.

\*\*\*    Von Daniken, Erich. CHARIOTS OF THE GODS? Bantam pbk., 1971.

\*\*    Williams, Charles. WITCHCRAFT. Meridian pbk., 1967.

\*\*    Wolf, Leonard. A DREAM OF DRACULA. Popular Library pbk., n.d.

## III. RECENT OCCULT FICTION

\*\*\*    Cerf, Bennett A., ed. FAMOUS GHOST STORIES. Random House, 1944.

\*\*\*    Ghidalia, Vic, ed. EIGHT STRANGE TALES. Fawcett pbk., 1972.

\*\*    Ghidalia, Vic, ed. THE DEVIL'S GENERATION. Lancer pbk., 1973.

\*\*    Lovecraft, H.P. THE COLOUR OUT OF SPACE. Lancer pbk., 1964.

\*\*\*    Lovecraft, H.P. THE DUNWICH HORROR, intro. by August Derleth. Lancer pbk., 1963.

\*\*    Serling, Rod. NIGHT GALLERY. Bantam pbk., 1971.

** Serling, Rod. STORIES FROM THE TWILIGHT ZONE. Bantam pbk., 1960.

** WEIRD TALES magazine, ed., Sam Moskowitz. Published quarterly.


## B. NOVELS

*** Blatty, William P. THE EXORCIST. Bantam pbk., 1972.

* Buchanan, Marie. ANIMA. Fawcett pbk., 1973.

*** James, Henry. THE TURN OF THE SCREW AND OTHER STORIES. Penguin pbk., 1969.

** Leader, Mary. TRIAD. Bantam pbk., 1974.

*** Levin, Ira. ROSEMARY'S BABY. Dell pbk., 1967.

** Marasco, Robert. BURNT OFFERINGS. Dell pbk., 1974.

*** Shelley, Mary. FRANKENSTEIN. New American Library pbk., 1965.

** Stewart, Ramona, THE POSSESSION OF JOEL DELANEY. Little Brown, 1970.

*** Stoker, Bram. DRACULA. Dell pbk., 1965.

** Tryon, Thomas. THE OTHER. Fawcett pbk., 1971.

## THE OCCULT: (GENERAL)

DeHaan, Richard W. SATAN, SATANISM AND WITCHCRAFT. Grand Rapids, MI: Zondervan Publishing House. 1972.

Eliade, Mircea. OCCULTISM, WITCHCRAFT, AND CULTURAL FASHIONS. Chicago: University of chicago Press, 1976.

Fritscher, John. POPULAR WITCHCRAFT STRAIGHT FROM THE WITCH'S MOUTH. Bowling Green, OH: Bowling Green University Popular Press, 1972.

Hansen, Chadwick. WITCHCRAFT AT SALEM. New York: New American Library, 1969.

Hodson, Geoffrey. THE HIDDEN WISDOM IN THE HOLY BIBLE, Vol. I. Wheaton, IL: The Theosophical Publishing House, 1967.

Hodson, Geoffrey. THE HIDDEN WISDOM IN THE HOLY BIBLE, Vol. II. Wheaton, IL: The Theosophical Publishing House, 1967.

Hodson, Geoffrey. THE HIDDEN WISDOM IN THE HOLY BIBLE, Vol. III. Wheaton, IL: The Theosophical Publishing House, 1971.

Hoeller, Stephan A. THE ROYAL ROAD. Wheaton, IL: The Theosophical Publishing House, 1975.

Hughes, Pennethorne. WITCHCRAFT. Baltimore: Penguin Books, 1969.

Kelsey, Morton T. THE CHRISTIAN AND THE SUPERNATURAL. Minneapolis: Augsburg Publishing House, 1976.

Cluff, Charles E. PARAPSYCHOLOGY AND THE CHRISTIAN FAITH. Valley Forge: Judson Press, 1976.

LaVey, Anton S. THE SATANIC BIBLE. New York: Avon Books, 1969.

Michelet, Jules. SATANISM AND WITCHCRAFT. New York: The Citadel Press, 1962.

Shadowitz, Albert & Peter Walsh. THE DARK SIDE OF KNOWLEDGE: EXPLORING THE OCCULT. Reading, MA: Addison-Wesley Publishing Co., 1976.

Winner, Anna Kennedy. THE BASIC IDEAS OF OCCULT WISDOM. Wheaton ILL: The Theosophical Publishing House, 1977.

Lindsey, Hall. THE TERMINAL GENERATION. Old Tappan, NJ: Revell Co., 1976.

## OCCULT: (DISASTERS)

Gentry, Curt. THE LAST DAYS OF THE LATE, GREAT STATE OF CALIFORNIA. New York: Ballantine Books, 1968.

Russell, D.S. APOCALYPTIC: ANCIENT AND MODERN. Philadelphia: Fortress Press, 1978.

## OCCULT: (AND CHRISTIAN SECTARIANISM) (POSSESSION)

Blatty, William Peter. THE EXORCIST. New York: Bantam Books, 1974.

Montgomery, John W. DEMON POSSESSION. Minneapolis: Bethany Fellowship, 1976.

## ESP (PARAPSYCHOLOGY & OCCULT)

Cohen, Daniel. ESP: THE SEARCH BEYOND THE SENSES. New York: Harcourt Brace Jovanovich, Inc., 1973.

Rhine, J.B. THE REACH OF THE MIND. New York: William Sloane Association, 1962.

Smith, Susy. ESP. New York: Pyramid Books, 1962.

## OCCULT ON IMMORTALITY ("DEATH" EXPERIENCES: REINCARNATION):

Bernstein, Morey. THE SEARCH FOR BRIDEY MURPHY. New York: Avon Books, 1975.

Ford, Arthur. THE LIFE BEYOND DEATH. New York: Berkley Publishing Co., 1975.

Guirdham, Arthur. THE CATHARS AND REINCARNATION. Wheaton, IL: The Theosophical Publishing House, 1970.

Hanson, Virginia, ed. Karma: THE UNIVERSAL LAW OF HARMONY. Wheaton, IL: The Theosophical Publishing House, 1975.

Head, Joseph and S. L. Cranston, eds. REINCARNATION. Wheaton, IL: The Theosophical Publishing House, 1975.

Moody, Raymond A., Jr. LIFE AFTER LIFE. New York: Bantam Books, 1975.

Pike, James A. THE OTHER SIDE. New York: Dell Books, 1968.

Reyes, Benito F. SCIENTIFIC EVIDENCE OF THE EXISTENCE OF THE SOUL. Wheaton: Quest Books, 1970.

Stearn, Jess. A MATTER OF IMMORTALITY. New York: Atheneum Publishing Co., 1976.

Stearn, Jess. THE SEARCH FOR THE GIRL WITH THE BLUE EYES. New York: Doubleday & Co., 1968.

Stearn Jess. THE SEEKERS. New York: Doubleday & Co., 1969.

Stearn, Jess. YOGA, YOUTH AND REINCARNATION. New York: Doubleday, 1965.

Stevenson, Ian, M.D. TWENTY CASES SUGGESTIVE OF REINCARNATION. New York: American Society for Psychical Research, 1966.

Sullivan, Eileen. ARTHUR FORD SPEAKS FROM BEYOND. Greenwich, CT: Fawcett Books, 1975.

**OCCULT (EDGAR CAYCE & ARE, VA BEACH, VA.)**

Stearn, Jess. A PROPHET IN HIS OWN COUNTRY. New York: Ballantine Books, 1974.

**OCCULT: I-CHING)**

Van Over, Raymond, ed. I CHING. New York: New American Library, 1971.

**OCCULT (ASTRAL TRAVEL, OUT OF THE BODY EXPERIENCES):**

Black, David. ECSTASY: OUT-OF-THE-BODY EXPERIENCES. New York: Berkley Publishing, 1975.

Green, Celia, OUT-OF-THE-BODY EXPERIENCES. New York: Ballantine Books, 1968.

Powell, A.E. THE ASTRAL BODY. Wheaton: A Quest Book, 1965.

Powell, A.E. THE ETHERIC DOUBLE. Wheaton: A Quest Book, 1969.

## OCCULT (CLAIRVOYANCE):

Dykshoorn, M. B. MY PASSPORT SAYS CLAIRVOYANT. New York: Jove Books, 1978.

## OCCULT (ATLANTIS):

Berlitz, Charles. THE MYSTERY OF ATLANTIS. New York: Avon Books, 1969.

LeCamp, L. Sprague. LOST CONTINENTS. New York: Dover Publications, 1970.

Michell, John. THE VIEW OVER ATLANTIS. New York: Ballantine Books, 1969.

## OCCULT (PYRAMIDS):

Schul, Bill and Ed Pettit. THE PSYCHIC POWER OF PYRAMIDS. Greenwich, CT: Fawcett Books, 1976.

## OCCULT (UFOLOGY; ANCIENT ASTRONAUTS, SCI-FI CULTS):

Heinlein, Robert A. STRANGER IN A STRANGE LAND. New York: Berkley Books, 1961.

Peters, Ted. UFO'S - GOD'S CHARIOTS? Atlanta: John Knox Press, 1977.

Von Daniken, Erich. CHARIOTS OF THE GODS? New York: Bantam Books, 1971.

Von Daniken, Erich. GODS FROM OUTER SPACE. New York: Bantam Books, 1971.

Wilson, Clifford, CRASH GO THE CHARIOTS. New York: Lancer Books, 1972.

## SECTARIAN AND OCCULT: (FAITH HEALING)

Regush, Nicholas, M. FRONTIERS OF HEALING: NEW DIMENSIONS IN PARAPSYCHOLOGY. New York: Avon Books, 1977.

Schul, Bill. THE PSYCHIC FRONTIERS OF MEDICINE. Greenwich: Fawcett books, 1977.

Simson, Eve. THE FAITH HEALER. St. Louis: Concordia Publishing House, 1977.

**OCCULT (ASTROLOGY):**

Reid, Vera W. TOWARDS AQUARIUS. New York: Arco Publishing Company, 1971.

Stearn, Jess. A TIME FOR ASTROLOGY. New York: New American Library, 1972.

**IMPORTANT STUDIES RELATING TO CULTISM:**

Braden, William, THE AGE OF AQUARIUS. New York: Pocket Books, 1971.

Filler, Louis, VANGUARDS AND FOLLOWERS. Chicago: Nelson-Hall, 1979.

Greeley, Andrew M. ECSTASY: A WAY OF KNOWING. Englewood Cliffs: Prentice-Hall, 1974.

Johnson, William A. THE SEARCH FOR TRANSCENDENCE. New York: Harper & Row, 1974.

Lanternari, Vittorio. THE RELIGIONS OF THE OPPRESSED. New York: New American Library, 1965.

Leonard, George B. EDUCATION AND ECSTASY. New York: Dell Publishing Company, 1968.

Margolis, Jack S. and Richard Clorfene. A CHILD'S GARDEN OF GRASS. New York: Ballantine Books, 1975.

Miller, David L. THE NEW POLYTHEISM. New York: Harper & Row, 1974.

Miller, Maul M. THE DEVIL DID NOT MAKE ME DO IT. Scottdale, PA: Herald Press, 1977.

McElveen, Floyd. THE MORMON REVELATIONS OF CONVENIENCE. Minneapolis: Bethany Fellowship, 1978.

Naranjo, Claudio. THE HEALING JOURNEY. New York: Ballantine Books, 1973.

Niebuhr, H. Richard. THE SOCIAL SOURCES OF DENOMINATIONALISM. Cleveland: The World Publishing Co., 1962.

Patrick, Ted. LET OUR CHILDREN GO! New York: Ballantine Books, 1976.

Robbins, Tom. ANOTHER ROADSIDE ATTRACTION. New York: Ballantine Books, 1971.

Smith, Adam. POWERS OF MIND. New York: Ballantine Books, 1975.

Watts, Alan W. PSYCHOTHERAPY EAST & WEST. New York: Ballantine Books, 1961.

Wilson, Howard A. INVASION FROM THE EAST. Minneapolis: Augsburg Publishing House, 1978.

## (WORLDWIDE CHURCH OF GOD) CULTS

Armstrong, Garner Ted. THE REAL JESUS. New York: Avon Books, 1977.

## VEDANTA:

Isherwood, Christopher, ed. VEDANTA FOR MODERN MAN. New York: Collier Books, 1962.

Morgan, Kenneth W. THE RELIGION OF THE HINDUS. New York: Ronald Press, 1953.

Vatsyayana. KAMA SUTRA: THE HINDU RITUAL OF LOVE. New York: Castle Books, 1963.

Sharma, I.C. ETHICAL PHILOSOPHIES OF INDIA, Lincoln, NE: Johnsen Publishing Company, 1965.

## ZEN:

Dell, R.F.S., Trans. ZEN by Eugen Herrigel. New York: McGraw-Hill, 1964.

Morgan, Kenneth W. THE PATH OF THE BUDDHA. New York: Ronald Press, 1956.

Watts, Alan W. THE WAY OF ZEN. New York: New American Library, 1961.

## SUFISM: (ISLAMIC MYSTICISM)

Arberry, A.J. SUFISM: AN ACCOUNT OF THE MYSTICS OF ISLAM. New York: Harper Torchbooks, 1970.

## BUDDHISM:

Amore, Roy C. TWO MASTERS, ONE MESSAGE. Nashville: Abingdon PRess, 1978.

Fausset, Hugh I. THE FLAME AND THE LIGHT, Wheaton, IL: Quest Books, 1976.

Humphreys, Christmas. BUDDHISM. Baltimore: Penguin Books, 1971.

Jacobson, Nolan Pliny. BUDDHISM: THE RELIGION OF ANALYSIS. Carbondale, IL: Southern Illinois University Press, 1970.

## CULTS: THE WAY

Wierwille, Victor Paul. THE WAY OF VICTOR PAUL WIERWILLE. Downers Grove, IL: InterVarsity Press, 1978.

## CULTS: HARE KRISHNA

Yamamoto, J. Isamu. HARE KRISHNA, HARE KRISHNA. Downers Grove, IL: InterVarsity Press, 1978.

## ADDENDUM:

THE OCCULT (Life after Death: Reincarnation)

Challoner, H. K. THE WHEEL OF REBIRTH. Wheaton, IL: Quest Books, 1976.

Greeley, Andrew. DEATH AND BEYOND. Chicago: Thomas More Association, 1976.

**THE OCCULT (GENERAL):**

Crowley, Aleister. MAGIC: IN THEORY AND PRACTICE. New York: Dover Publications, 1976.

Kramer, Heinrich & James Sprenger. THE MALLEUS MALEFICAR-UM. New York: Dover Publications, 1971.

Scot, Reginald. THE DISCOVERIES OF WITCHCRAFT. New York: Dover Publications, 1972.

Siberer, Herbert. HIDDEN SYMBOLISM OF ALCHEMY AND THE OCCULT ARTS. New York: Dover Publications, 1971.

(The Reader is Invited to Interview Him/Her self.)

## QUESTIONNAIRE

1. Are you interested in the Occult, Spiritualism and/or Mysticism? Answer yes or no and why.



2. If so, how long have you been interested?

3. Where did you first become introduced to Occult matters? When? By whom were you introduced?



4. Do you really believe in the predictive or analytic powers of the Tarot, Palmistry, numbers, the crystal ball, etc? Why or why not?



5. How do you explain your belief -- or misbelief?

6.   Are you Christian or Jewish?

7.   If so, what denomination?

8.   Do you attend church regularly?  How much religious instruction have you had?

9.   How do you harmonize your religious belief and belief in the Occult?

10.  Do you think of yourself as extremely (or very) religious?

11.  Have you ever had a "Born Again" experience?

12.  If so, when and what were the circumstances?

13.  If you are not religious, or, at least, do not attend services, do you, nevertheless, believe in God?

14.  Have you ever had a supernatural (Occult, "spooky") experience?  If so, please detail.

15. What do you feel is the major achievement you wish to accomplish in your life?




16. Age

17. Sex

18. Educational Attainment

19. Name (optional)

20. Marital Status

# BIOGRAPHICAL STATEMENT

John Charles Cooper is Professor of Religion and Chairman of the Department of Philosophy and Religion at Susquehanna University, Selinsgrove, Pennsylvania. Previously he was Dean of Academic Affairs, Winebrenner Theological Seminary, Findlay, Ohio; Professor of Philosophy and Chairman, Department of Philosophy, Eastern Kentucky University; and Professor of Philosophy and Chairman, Department of Philosophy, Newberry College, in South Carolina. He is an Ordained Lutheran Minister, and has served churches in Pennsylvania, Ohio, Kentucky, South Carolina and Florida. he is a graduate of the University of South Carolina (AB), The Lutheran Theological Southern Seminary (M.Div.), The Lutheran School of Theology at Chicago (STM), and the University of Chicago (MA and Ph.D.). His Ph.D. was a study of his teacher, Paul Tillich's Doctrine of the Spirit. Cooper is the author, co-author or editor of thirty books, including: THE ROOTS OF THE RADICAL THEOLOGY; THE NEW MENTALITY; RELIGION IN THE AGE OF AQUARIUS; CELULOID AND SYMBOLS; RELIGION AFTER FORTY; FINDING A SIMPLER LIFE; FANTASY AND THE HUMAN SPIRIT; LIVING, LOVING AND LETTING GO; WHY WE HURT AND WHO CAN HEAL; NOT FOR A MILLION DOLLARS; THE JOY OF THE PLAIN LIFE; RELIGIOUS PIED PIPERS; and DEALING WITH DESTRUCTIVE CULTS. His articles have appeared in AUGUSTINIAN STUDIES, THE BUCKNELL REVIEW, THE LUTHERAN QUARTERLY, THE LUTHERAN, THE SOUTHERN HUMANITIES REVIEW, CHRISTIANITY TODAY, THE SOUTHERN JOURNAL OF PHILOSOPHY and THE CLERGY JOURNAL. Cooper is a frequent bookreviewer for THE CHRISTIAN CENTURY and THE JOURNAL OF ECUMENICAL STUDIES. The research for his writing has been funded by grants from The Danforth Foundation, The Ohio Program in The Humanities, The Connecticut Humanities council, The National Endowment For The Humanities, The Kentucky State Universities Research Council and The Lutheran Church in America.